The Endangered Ones

The Endangered Ones

by James A. Cox

A Rutledge Book
Crown Publishers, Inc.
New York

Fred R. Sammis — Director
John T. Sammis — Creative Director
Doris Townsend — Editor-in-Chief
Allan Mogel — Art Director
Sally Andrews — Managing Editor
Mimi Koren — Associate Editor
Jeremy Friedlander — Associate Editor
B. G. Murphy — Associate Editor
Arthur Gubernick — Production Consultant
Annemarie Bosch — Production Manager
Elyse Shick — Associate Art Director
Eric Marshall — Art Associate
Jay Hyams — Assistant Editor

For Michael, who loves animals

Destroyed buildings can be rebuilt; destroyed works of art may possibly be replaced by new creations; but every animal and every flower which becomes extinct is lost forever in the most absolute of all deaths.

—Joseph Wood Krutch

Library of Congress Catalog Card Number: 75-7534
ISBN: 0-517-521598

Prepared and produced by Rutledge Books, 25 West 43 Street, New York, N.Y. 10036.
Published in 1975 by Crown Publishers, Inc., 419 Park Avenue South, New York, N.Y. 10016.
Printed in Italy by Mondadori, Verona.
First printing.

Contents

In the Beginning

When I was a boy, a couple of friends and I used to have some wonderful arguments about Noah and the Ark. We debated whether or not the story was true, of course, and, if so, how big Noah would have had to build the craft in order to fit all the creatures in. We also questioned whether insects were included, and how he went about gathering up all the animals, especially those that weren't too friendly, and what he fed them on that long voyage while waiting for the waters to subside.

This last item brought up the biggest and best argument of all. For although the Bible account states that God commanded Noah to bring along food for his family and the animal passengers, there wasn't a one of us in that group of boys who doubted for a minute what would happen if you crowded a bunch of lions, tigers, leopards, bears, wolves, and snakes on the same boat with cows and sheep and rabbits and antelopes—not to mention people—and they got loose.

The big question in our argument was who would be the winner—which creature would stand among the bones of his victims, the last survivor, by the time that lonely Ark beached on the soggy land? The lions and tigers had most of the backers, and one smart kid held out for the rat. But, strangely enough, not one of the boys in that hot debate believed that Noah or his family would emerge victorious. In the confined, unnatural world of the Ark, surrounded by ferocious beasts and with no place to run to, we didn't see how any person, unless he were armed with a submachine gun, could survive.

How wrong we were! For we are beginning to realize now that the earth itself is really an Ark, on a somewhat larger scale than Noah's, to be sure, but still a confined, limited vessel. And we are also coming to understand that human kind, the most successful and most dangerous species that ever existed, is proliferating and expanding its activities at such a rate that the day may come when there is no room on this Ark for anything but us and the creatures we decide we need—dogs and cats for companionship (and perhaps to salve our consciences), and cows, pigs, sheep,

chickens, and other protein sources to fill the gaping maws of billions of hungry people.

Most of the world's problems today in ecology and conservation stem from the fact that humans have almost always considered themselves better than their fellow creatures, and as a consequence have taken care of their own needs and wants first—and often enough to the exclusion of all others. The statement has to be qualified with the word "almost," because there was a time, many ages ago, when the superiority of human beings was in question, and none but the shrewdest and most far-seeing of gamblers would have put money on them. After all, they couldn't run or swim very fast, they couldn't fly at all, they had no carapace for protection, their teeth were dull, and their fingernails were weak. Some of the things they did have, though, were worth all those other qualities combined—fingers with opposing thumbs, for example, which enabled them to pick up stones and use them as tools or weapons, and imaginative, creative brains, which told them how to put their useful hands to work.

And so, with stones and sticks as the first great equalizers, men set out to prove that they were considerably more than just coresidents of the earth—that they were, in fact, the rulers of it. It took a long time for this idea to coalesce in the human brain, of course, for in the earliest years of their evolutionary growth their main concern was to protect themselves from stronger, more agile hunters and to find enough food to satisfy their pangs of hunger. But as their weapons and hunting techniques improved, they became more than matches for their prey, and for their hunting competitors, too, despite the huge size some of these attained. Spears, bows and arrows, boomerangs, blowpipes, bone knives, stone axes, fish hooks, snares, fish traps made of rushes and vines, all combined to turn human beings into efficient killers—so efficient that they very likely exterminated many of the larger species of animals that inhabited the world. This was perhaps their first major impact on their environment, and a precursor of things to come.

As game became scarce in one area, people had to move on to more fruitful fields,

Preceding pages:
page 1
Orangutan
James H. Carmichael, Jr.

pages 2-3
Slender-horned gazelle
San Diego Zoo

pages 6-7
Komodo dragon
Bruce Coleman Inc.

and so the pattern of migrations was established. In time, they discovered that certain animals could be collected, controlled, and bred, assuring them of supplies of milk and meat and relieving them of the necessity of being full-time hunters and foragers. But now that they were herders, their migrations were more necessary than ever. And as the nomad herds ate their way across the land, stripping surface vegetation and destroying roots, some of the drier areas eventually deteriorated into deserts—probably the second major impact of organized man on his environment.

But this was nothing compared with what was to follow. About 8000 B.C., in the so-called fertile crescent of the Middle East, the first people settled down to a life of tilling the soil. Now everything began to change. Some people became artisans and traders. Clusters of huts became villages, and the villages grew into towns and cities. Modern civilization was on its way, sustained and nourished by an ever-spreading advance guard of farms.

Humans now began to reshape their pristine world with relentless intent, for agriculture needs fields, not forests, pastures, not marshes. The term "habitat destruction" never entered anyone's head, but the effects of the process were already at work, driving the larger wild animals farther and farther from human domain. For some of them, the inevitable result was oblivion: there is little doubt that the Asiatic lion started on its long walk down the road to extinction in the Middle East and Europe at the same time that the first primitive farmers were clearing the land with fire and ax, and planting crops of wheat and barley.

It is unlikely that the earliest people, caught between hunger and fear, thought much, if at all, about their role in nature. But with the sense of security and satisfaction that came as their herds grew, and then their farms, they had time to consider the fact that they were now preeminent among the creatures of the world. With the refinement of civilization, this idea swelled into arrogance, and now people were able to convince themselves that there was no other purpose for the rest of Creation but to serve them and their needs. Fortifying this belief, they wrote in the Bible, and then frequently quoted: "And God blessed them, saying: Increase and multiply, and fill the earth, and subdue it, and rule over the fishes of the sea, and the fowls of the air, and all living creatures that move upon the earth."

So, in the name of God—and later in the name of the new deity, Progress—people set about "taming the wilds" and "conquering nature." It was a painfully slow process at first, for the world seemed huge and human numbers were comparatively few. As a result, they barely scratched the surface, in a literal sense, and for thousands of years lived in incomplete but reasonable harmony with their world.

Then came the rise of modern Western civilization from the cradle of the Middle Ages, and the world was never to be the same again. Braving the terrors of the unknown in their cocky—and leaky—little wooden ships, the Portuguese and Spanish "discovered" the rest of the world, even though the Phoenicians, Vikings, Polynesians, and other early navigators had got there first. Rubbing their palms together over the prospect of untold riches, the explorers—the British, French, and Dutch were into the act, too—raced around claiming the virgin lands in the name of this or that king or queen, regardless of the opinions of the inhabitants. Another migratory wave, this time of colonists, gained a toehold in the wild lands of the world, bringing with them some of the benefits of European civilization—and most of its problems. And now the taming and conquering of nature went forward with a vengeance, for in addition to their plows and axes, Westerners carried the ultimate symbol of their mastery over other forms of life—the gun.

This was bad enough; but from the point of view of nature, worse was to come. For Western people were even now embarking on a venture that would drastically alter the tenor and tempo of their lives, and would eventually have an overwhelming impact on the entire world. The Industrial Revolution, born in England in the eighteenth century, can be considered either as cornucopia or Pandora's box, and perhaps a little too much of both. As the factories proliferated, men, women, and children left the fields to work in gloomy sweatshops and "dark satanic mills," or descended deep into the earth to pluck out its ores, tending machines until they were little better than machines themselves. But there was a trade-off of sorts—merchandise poured forth, and the workers were able to exchange their earnings for at least a taste of the new-found "good things in life."

The machine age grew and flourished, particularly in the Western world, to be joined more recently by the age of technology. The results certainly haven't been all bad. We have machines that relieve us of tedious and onerous chores, we can communicate with each other in a twinkling, we have more leisure time and a multitude of interesting ways in which to spend it, we have bountiful crops and, through advances in medicine and drugs, the prospect of a longer, richer, fuller life than any people in history has ever enjoyed.

But in the process of gaining these blessings, we have inflicted serious hurts on our world, and on the other creatures inhabiting it with us. Through ignorance, greed, and carelessness, we have destroyed or wasted millions of square miles of woodlands, wetlands, and grasslands. We have exterminated scores of animal species for their meat, hides, and feathers, or simply because they competed with us for food and space. And unwittingly or thoughtlessly, we are driving countless other creatures to the brink of extinction through the rampant spread of our civilization.

The world has gone through a number of "crunches" in recent years, so the situation we're concerned with here could reasonably be called the "habitat crunch." It is not limited to one country, one area, or one continent. Europe, highly developed over the centuries, has already gone through the process; Britain, with the peculiar vulnerability of island ecosystems, is practically devoid of the higher forms of wildlife, an example of what the future may hold. The United States, although it sometimes seems to think of itself still as a frontier land, will soon be like Europe, if not England, unless the tide is reversed. Recent computer studies project a United States in the year 2000 with only a few scattered areas where wildlife, in severely diminished numbers, can be expected to survive.

San Diego Zoo

Przewalski's horse

But the greatest impact today is being felt in the underdeveloped nations of the globe, the last bastions of many forms of wildlife. Through the marvels of modern science and medicine, infant mortality in these lands is being reduced and life-spans extended, with the result that population figures are surging even while the more developed countries are trying to limit their population growth. In the simplest of terms, what this means is a corresponding surge in human needs—for more food, more space, more homes, more *things*. As a consequence, the last great forests in Africa, South America, and Asia are falling before the bulldozers of the developers and the chain saws of the lumbermen; wetlands are being drained or filled in to make way for new suburbs or industrial complexes; the farmer's

plow is biting deeper and deeper into the savannas and hillsides; and the wastes of civilization are beginning to poison once-clear lakes and streams—a noose of human activity drawing ever tighter about the wild creatures sharing these regions.

This is not an overstatement of the case. The noted ornithologist Roger Tory Peterson has predicted that "we will soon lose more species in the American tropics, particularly in the fast-disappearing forests of the northern Andes, than in any other part of the world. And most of them will go with no one taking note of their passing." Even sadder, says Dr. Thomas Lovejoy of the World Wildlife Fund, there are creatures now living in those forests that will go into extinction without anyone even having known they existed.

The situation is a difficult one to resolve, for who is to say that the peoples of the newly developing lands have less right to do for—and to—themselves what we in the industrialized nations have already done? On the other hand, it would be a matter of overwhelming shortsightedness if they did not profit by our mistakes. In some enlightened lands, measures have already been taken to set aside reserves where indigenous wildlife can live to some extent as nature intended them to. Great efforts must be made to persuade other nations to do the same. If we fail in this, we face a bleak and lonely future, for our fellow creatures are, in the words of the late William Morton Wheeler, "our only companions in an infinite and unsympathetic waste of electrons, planets, nebulae, and stars."

To What End?

There is a deep sense of sadness in the definition of the word *extinct:* "not existing now, that has ended or died out, no longer in use, obsolete, extinguished, quenched, gone, vanished. See *dead.*"

But with *exterminate,* the mood turns dark and insane: "to get rid of by destroying, destroy totally, extirpate, eradicate, abolish, annihilate, eliminate."

Since the beginning of life on earth, untold numbers of animal and plant species have gone into extinction, losers, in a manner of speaking, in the evolutionary race. The great saurians rose to ascendancy, flourished for more than 100 million years, then declined as the world grew colder. Giant mammals once trod the earth, huge birds, too, many of them flightless, and eventually passed into oblivion. No species has survived for more than a few million years unchanged, for the inexorable rule of the evolutionary game is simple: adapt or die. So the successful forms adapted, mutated, while the weaker ones faded away; new shoots sprouted from the best of the old, and in the harsh process of natural selection the quality of organic life became enriched.

There are many things that can bring about the extinction of a race or species—over-specialization, for example, or the pressure of one creature on another, either as a predator or as a stronger and better-adapted competitor for the same food or habitat. Natural phenomena, such as volcanic upheavals, floods, and earthquakes, can destroy localized races, and long-term changes in climate and the patient sculpturing of wind and water can make life untenable. In nature's way, most environmental changes of major import occur over millions of years, allowing enough time for successful adaptations to take place—time necessary, since the adaptations, being products of mutations, must go through a lengthy series of experiments.

But the human coming of age injected a new element into the game of survival, not merely because humans are the most wanton predators of all time—exterminators on a wholesale scale—but also because their unthinking alterations of the environment take place so rapidly that there is no time for natural forces to react. There are some who callously refer to this as "survival of the fittest." But fitness has little to do with it, unless we take the supremely arrogant view that human beings, being the fittest of all by virtue of technology and the trappings of civilization, have a right to do whatever they want with and to the other, "lesser" creatures in the world.

Judged by our actions, this is pretty much the view we have adopted. Since 1600, more or less the beginning of the modern era, about 120 forms of mammals and 150 forms of birds have traveled the road to extinction, from which there is no return. These do not appear as staggering figures when we learn that, in 1600, there were an estimated 4,226 species of mammals and 8,684 species of birds inhabiting the planet. But it is sobering to learn that only a quarter of the animals lost went out of existence through natural causes: the rest, the overwhelming majority, were exterminated —directly or indirectly—by man. Since this carnage took place in the course of less than four hundred years, rather than the hundreds of thousands or millions that nature allots, it raises the question of just what we have in

San Diego Zoo

Red uakari

Preceding pages:
Yellow-footed rock wallaby
Australian Information Service Photograph by D. McNaughton

mind when we talk of taming the wilds and conquering nature.

Most frightening is the fact that the tempo of annihilation is quickening. In the case of the birds, about ten disappeared in the seventeenth century, twenty in the eighteenth century, twenty more in the first half of the nineteenth century, and about one hundred in the century and a quarter since. Add in the 120 missing mammals, plus those we know that disappeared before 1600, and we find that the world lost an average of two animal species every hundred years for the first eighteen centuries of the Christian era; after that the pace began to mount rapidly, so that our record in this cenutry works out to one species destroyed *every year.*

Shocking? Then consider the scope of the potential tragedy that lies ahead. The majestic tiger, the giant blue whale, the intelligent orangutan, the peregrine falcon, the California condor, the polar bear, are all standing in the shadow of extinction. So are more than seven hundred other birds, mammals, reptiles, and fishes, many of which are not expected to survive the present century. And the official "doomsday lists" include only those animals that scientists know about. How many more obscure and elusive creatures— the inhabitants of the sea, for example, and insects, rodents, and other unpopular "little uglies"—have disappeared or are on their way out is anybody's guess, for only now are attempts being made to determine their condition. Plants, too, have received little attention, yet we know that preliminary estimates put 20,000 species throughout the world in danger from the march of man.

Many nations are now keeping their own lists of endangered species, but the most comprehensive is the *Red Data Book* compiled and updated regularly by the International Union for Conservation of Nature and Natural Resources (IUCN) from its headquarters in Morges, Switzerland. Putting together reports from field correspondents and scientific study teams, the *Red Book* (red for danger) provides in capsule form all that is known as of a given date about the status of each animal included —an estimate of how many are left, the areas in which they have been observed, the apparent

reasons for their decline, what remedial action can be or is being taken, and their prospects for survival.

The *Red Book* has been called the "basic data bank of wildlife conservation," and although the evidence presented under each entry is not always equal in weight and value, the sum bears out the observation that human activities are now responsible for a greater percentage of animals in trouble than ever before. What the statistics are saying is that our contribution to the eradication of our fellow creatures—75 percent in the period from 1600 to the present—will rise to 87 percent and higher if we continue on the way we are going.

But there is a serious question as to whether we can stop the way we are going. What are we doing that's so bad? A quick and capricious answer might be that we are just being ourselves. First and foremost, we continue to breed at such a rate that some observers foresee the time when there will be no room on the earth for anything but human beings—and then not enough room for them. Fortunately, we are not close to the crash-peak of the exponential population curve yet. Recent

Gladys Porter Zoo

Hooded crane

15

estimates maintain that the entire population of the world could fit into Baltimore County, Maryland—the catch being, of course, that we would be jammed in shoulder to shoulder.

Still, the population of the human species is growing at an accelerated rate, and the point is not how many bodies we can squeeze into a given area of the earth's surface, but how much of that surface, with its resources, is required to sustain each body. If, in order to build their own comfortable habitats, the relatively "scant" populations of the historical past and present had to cut down two-thirds of the world's forests, drain its marshes for urban subdivisions, convert its rolling prairies into farmland, turn its streams into open sewers, and convert its lakes and oceans into monstrous dumps, what hope is there that the surging populations of the future will be able to spare any living space for wildlife, even if they only have to stand fingertip to fingertip rather than shoulder to shoulder?

Loss of a natural habitat is usually—though not always—followed by loss of the creatures that lived there. To survive and flourish, all forms of life need an environment in which they can find food, water, and oxygen, avoid predators and disease, eliminate waste products without despoiling that environment, find mates and reproduce. When their natural environment is destroyed or drastically altered, they must move on, adapt, or face elimination in the competition of life.

Habitat destruction, then, is the most serious threat to wildlife in the near and distant future. Since it is, in a way, unintentional, it could be defended on the grounds that the needs of human beings are higher on the priority list—although the ivory-billed woodpecker, Mexican grizzly, pygmy chimpanzee, white-tailed gnu, and a host of others might well ask, were they able, "Whose list?" But the second exterminating force in the human arsenal—intentional slaughter, including hunting, commercial exploitation, and the eradication of so-called "pests" and "vermin"—is totally indefensible on all grounds except ego and profits.

Before hunters and fishermen rise up in wrath, let us hasten to add the adjective

indiscriminate. Many sportsmen's and fishery associations are in the forefront of the movement to preserve wildlife, and if their motivation is primarily to ensure an adequate supply of targets for their rifles, lures, and nets, and their efforts are expended only on behalf of certain creatures, this does not reduce the value of their contribution. Men like Theodore Roosevelt and George Bird Grinnell cannot be faulted because their conservation vision was clouded by mounted heads and stuffed birds. The fact that they saw the need for some kind of conservation as clearly as they did at a time in history when most of the rest of mankind was blind should be cause for rejoicing.

Hunting may hurt the sensibilities of those who believe any kind of killing is obscene. But wildlife specialists believe that controlled hunting, in which excess animals are cropped periodically, is best for a herd in the long run when habitat is limited and natural predators, which usually take the weak, sick, and aged, are few. And although the right to kill by official sanction may be considered a special form of barbarism, we must remember that man was a hunter before he was a philosopher, and atavistic memories linger longer in some than in others. If we had remained vegetarians eons ago—our grinding molars give us away—there probably would be no hunters today. But we developed a taste for flesh, so much so that today we raise and consume billions of pounds of beef, chicken, lamb, veal, and pork every year, the difference between us and our ancestors being that we do most of our hunting at the meat counter, looking for bargains.

So there is reason to accept hunting of plentiful species under certain conditions. But there is no excuse for the hunter who slays a rare animal in order to mount its head on the wall, or the "sportsman" who shoots polar bears from helicopters, timber wolves from snowmobiles, and Arabian oryxes from limousines. The hungry primitive tribesman in Africa can be forgiven if he doesn't understand why it is wrong for him to hunt the white rhinoceros, as his forefathers did for ages, to bring home meat to his family. But it is less forgivable when he slays the great beast and leaves the meat to rot, selling only the horn for the money it will bring because somewhere an aging Chinese gentleman feels the need of an aphrodisiac, which ground rhino horn is reputed to be. The crime is compounded when he sneaks into a game reserve where he knows the animals are protected; but this is no worse than the actions of better-educated poachers, who almost succeeded in wiping out the American alligator and many of the big cats to satisfy the dictates of fashion.

How do you convince ranchers and stockmen that it is better to lose an occasional calf or chicken than to take off after bald eagles in private planes or set out poisoned bait for the coyote and other "vermin"—or any other meat-eater that happens along? If people who own pets really love animals, aren't they disturbed when they read that wild horses and whales are being ground out of existence just to feed millions of pampered cats and dogs? How do Russian and Japanese whalers justify their refusal to limit catches of already scarce whale species in accordance with international agreements?

Add to these depredations, and so many others like them, the actual and potential killing capabilities of pesticides and chemical wastes from our high-powered civilization, and the picture becomes grim indeed. We are a talented species, but sometimes our ability to think betrays us. Sometimes we forget our origins, forget that we are animals, too, and therefore are just as vulnerable to our own deadly inventions as other creatures. If birds and fish and mammals are affected adversely by our poisons, to the extent that many of them are dying off, do we really think we can remain forever immune, or reduce nature's adaptation rate down to a decade or two? The things we are doing to the world are changing it so rapidly that only the hardiest—and perhaps the least desirable—creatures will be able to adapt. And that brings up an interesting question.

Biologists tell us that the web of all life is interrelated, that everything that lives is part of the food chain, that all things are interdependent. Some years ago in California, stockmen set out poisoned bait for coyotes, and in the process managed to kill off most of the predator animals in the area. A few months later, hordes of mice swept across the countryside in an all-consuming wave, eating everything in sight and causing millions of dollars worth of damage. Only recently it was reported that insects had proliferated alarmingly in some areas of Europe because pollution in ponds was killing off the frogs. In parts of South America and Africa where the big cats have been eradicated, rat populations have boomed and jungle villages have been ravaged with disease. In yet another case, nasty parasites that once preyed on hippos had to find a new host when the animals were sorely depleted. They found one—human beings.

Evolutionary change, adaptation, relies on mutation of the genes, which is passed on from generation to generation. It stands to reason, then, that the creature with the shortest gestation period, the quickest maturation rate, and the most prolific reproduction rate will have a better chance of mutating—adapting—quickly. The mayfly is born, reproduces, and dies in a day. Two mice can overpopulate a tenement district in a year. The gestation period for man is nine months and for the elephant considerably longer, with one offspring the usual result. Which has an edge in the evolutionary odds? If there's any doubt, recall that DDT, considered so dangerous that the United States banned it in 1971, became ineffective against many species of insects within a relatively few generations.

In our search for a better life for ourselves, we are severely disturbing the fragile web that holds all life together, and we don't know what the results will be if we cut too many strands. This world is our habitat, too, the only one we're sure of, and we sometimes forget that damage done to our habitat is damage done to ourselves—and to *our* prospects for avoiding extinction. There are many birds and reptiles that eat their weight in insects every day. There are snakes and coyotes and other "vermin" that keep the rodent population in check. Without their assistance, can we be absolutely certain that, in any long-run battle for survival, we will prove fitter to inherit the earth than rats and mice, and flies, mosquitoes, cockroaches, and their multitude of kin, already the most numerous creatures in the world?

Making Room in the Ark

Of all the creatures in the world, humans alone have the power to think rationally. Only they have had the ability to alter the world. And only they have the power to undo what they have done.

There is still hope for wildlife, still time to reverse the tide of destruction, to keep our consciences clear of the ultimate outrage against our world, to prove that, since we have taken upon ourselves the function of ruling the earth, we are capable of ruling it wisely and with compassion. But time is running out.

There was a time when migrating passenger pigeons blotted out the sun in North America, when bison by the millions thundered across the western prairies, when the beautiful quagga darkened the South African veldt, when sea otters, smallest of the marine mammals, turned the coastal waters of the northern Pacific into a playground. Then came the hunters and trappers. The quagga is lost, the passenger pigeon will pass this way no more. But the bison has been saved, in the nick of time, and the sea otter family, once thought to be so far gone it could never recover, is now up to almost 50,000 members.

The annals of wildlife history contain many such stories, with the failures, unhappily, outnumbering the successes. But the successes do show what can be done if people of common sense cooperate in common cause. And it isn't as if there were no precedent for protecting rare and endangered species, even though we seem to have forgotten the lessons of the past.

In the introduction to *Wildlife in Danger,* the late James Fisher, commissioner of the IUCN's Survival Service, wrote:

At some time in their evolution, many Stone Age groups encountered the effects of their own Pleistocene over-kill and developed lore of totem, taboo, and self-denying ordinance, cropping and rationing rules. . . . The Persian kings of old enclosed little wildernesses of hunting land and called them paradises, and the Norman kings of England did the same and called them parks and chases. The Zulu King Dingaan, himself no mean hunter of elephants and trader in ivory, estab-lished a protected game park years before the present game-park system was developed in Africa. . . . The Vikings of a thousand years ago or more established a sea-bird hunting culture in St. Kilda and other parts of the Hebrides, and in Faeroe and Iceland . . . with very strict rules about the cropping season and the size of the 'take.' . . . This wisdom appears to have been widely forgotten again in our later years of post-Renaissance exploration, and particularly since the Industrial Revolution, and the rapid refine-ment of guns and other hunting tools, in the early 19th century.

In early America, twelve of the thirteen colonies had to establish closed seasons on deer because of overkill, and Massachusetts passed laws regulating the catch of some fish during the spawning season, not for conservation but because it was believed that roe-laden fish were of inferior quality and would injure the reputation of the fish merchants. But most American laws pertaining to wildlife were primarily concerned with offering bounties for wolves, foxes, and other "pests," and the killing went on until a high point was reached between 1890 and 1910. In this short period, all around the world, the number of bird and mammal species going into extinction reached epidemic proportions.

Not everyone was shocked, not everyone cared, but enough conservationists exerted enough pressure, reached enough ears, to start whittling away at public and governmental indifference. In 1900, the Lacey Act made it a federal offense to ship birds killed in violation of state laws across state lines. In 1903, President Theodore Roosevelt set aside Pelican Island, on Florida's east coast, as a "preserve and breeding ground for native birds"—the first National Wildlife Refuge in the United States. The system has expanded steadily since then, and today, with 356 refuges encompassing 30 million acres scattered throughout the fifty states, it ranks as the largest network of managed wildlife areas in the world.

Earlier, back in 1872, the United States became the first nation to set up a national park —Yellowstone—and within a few decades Australia, Sweden, and other countries followed suit. Today there are thousands of such parks throughout the world, a boon to both humans and wildlife. Africa has many famous animal reserves, well-managed for the most part and valuable tourist attractions, bringing much-needed income to poor nations. Indonesia has set up reserves to protect the rare Javan rhinoceros, China has established a reserve for the giant panda, India has a park in the foothills of the Himalayas, where it hopes to save the tiger, Israel has a research station at Hai Bar devoted to reintroducing such endangered biblical animals as the addax, the scimitar-horned oryx, and the Persian onager where they haven't been seen for many years.

With so many parks and reserves already in existence, one might ask, why do we need more? Why not just fill the ones we have with the animals that are in trouble? There are many reasons why that wouldn't work, not the least of which is the danger implicit in introducing exotic species into an area where they are unknown. People have tried this in the past, with disastrous results, for often enough the arrival of the newcomer signals the end of the road for indigenous species, which are suddenly faced with a competitor or a predator they are not equipped to handle. The results, history shows, are especially devastating in limited ecosystems, such as islands—or wildlife reserves. But the overriding reason comes down to a matter of "ecological niche."

Life exists on earth only in a thin skin of air, water, and land, known as the biosphere: on land, roughly from the tops of the trees to the depths of their roots, and on the sea, from the surface to the bottom. The biosphere, in turn, is divided into biomes, which are geographical areas with distinctive characteristics of climate. There are nine major land biomes: desert, tundra, savanna, grassland, chaparral, woodland, deciduous forest, coniferous forest, and tropical rain forest. Each of these biomes has plant life peculiar to it alone, determined by such things as temperature, rainfall, and soil conditions, and the plant life, in turn, determines to a large extent which animals will live successfully there. They, both plants and animals, have found their ecological niche.

Through adaptation over billions of years, animals and plants have managed to fill just about every ecological niche in the biosphere. Koalas live in the tops of eucalyptus trees, where they dine on the tender young leaves. Several types of grazing animals can exist side by side in the same biome because some eat only new shoots, some prefer dry grass, some eat the tops, and some eat the stalks. Hippopotamuses earned their name, which means "river horse," because they spend much of their time in streams, feeding on aquatic plants.

Could a hippo survive in a desert biome? Would the cuddly koala find anything to eat on the prairie? How long would a herd of zebras last in a coniferous forest? Or a woodpecker on the treeless tundra? The point, obviously, is that, if we are going to take over most of the world for human activity, yet still want to save the flora and fauna that are an integral part of each biome, we must preserve for them the proper niche, or habitat, in which they fit.

There is a growing awareness of this need, and a willingness on the part of many nations to dedicate some of their space to the preservation of habitats for wild creatures. This awareness reached its highest point only in the past decade, however, when the world, suddenly waking up to the fact that it was in trouble in many ways, began to realize that the plight of its animal inhabitants might well be a falling barometer foretelling a coming storm for all of mankind.

In 1966, fighting the disinterest and outright ridicule of many of his colleagues, Senator Karl Mundt of South Dakota pushed an endangered species bill through the Congress of the United States. This landmark legislation, the first federal law exclusively devoted to the welfare of all endangered wildlife, pledges the United States "to conserve and protect, where practical, the various species of native fish and wildlife, including game and non-game migratory birds, that are threatened with extinction."

In 1970, a conference of concerned nations was held at Strasbourg, France, marking the beginning of the European Conservation Year. This was followed in 1972 by the first United Nations Conference of the Human Environment in Stockholm, Sweden, attended by delegates of 113 countries and by representatives from about 1,000 conservation-minded organizations. By no means an unqualified success, since the poorer nations attending were not at all convinced that they should put wildlife preservation higher on the priority list than economic development, the conference nevertheless provided a major first step toward cooperation in trying to solve the world's environmental problems. It also led to a belated recognition that the problems belong to the whole world, industrialized and underdeveloped nations alike, and cannot be handled in piecemeal fashion. "The earth is a closed ecological system," the delegates agreed, "and man continues to modify it only at his peril."

A year later, in 1973, representatives from eighty nations meeting in Washington, D.C., signed an agreement which, by exercising international control over wild animals and animal products, would serve to protect wildlife from exploitation. And at the end of the year the U.S. Congress passed the Endangered Species Act of 1973, expanding and strengthening the preceding statutes and for the first time providing funds for state programs. The act also directed the Secretary of the Smithsonian Institution "to review species of plants which are now or may become endangered or threatened and methods of adequately conserving such species."

Cynically, one might say that the road to extinction, like the road to hell, is paved with good intentions. The measures being taken and talked about will probably come too late to save many animals, especially those whose numbers are so few already. In 1971, Dr. Wolfgang Ullrich, director of the Dresden Zoo, listed these near-extinct populations: "150 Zanzibar marmosets, 3 or 4 Bali tigers, 150 panther-lynx, 50 Caribbean monk seals, 50 Chilean fur seals, 100 Sumatra elephants, 24 Java rhinoceroses, 82 Cape Mountain zebras, 150 Abyssinian ibex, 100 Cretan wild goats, 100 Arabian oryx antelopes, 50 to 100 giant eland, 50 to 60 Mesopotamian fallow deer."

But wildlife specialists are convinced—

Hunter's hartebeest

and they have much successful experience to back their confidence—that, given the proper facilities and funds for research, they can bring many species of animals out of danger and prevent others from falling into the ominous "red" zone. Elsewhere in this book, in addition to profiles of endangered animals, there are accounts of some of these bright spots in the life-saving crusade.

Despite our growing sense of conscience and the eagerness of many people both in and out of the scientific community to do something, there are still those selfish enough to say, "Why bother?" There is no use in appealing to them on esoteric grounds; no use in pointing out to them, as Robert Gray did so eloquently in a work for the San Diego Zoo's Wild Animal Park, that "wild animals, and the wild places they need in order to live, have the right to exist simply because they do exist. They have been our neighbors on this planet for two million years. They predate our relatively late arrival. And they are parts of the fabric which we call life. Pulling out any one of the parts can place the entire fabric in danger, for, in nature, all things are related to many other things. Mankind needs animals in the wilderness as living reminders of his past. Despite his technology and civilization, he is still very much a part of earth's natural processes. Wild animals can remind him of this. Even if he never sees them in the wilderness, there is comfort in knowing that they are out there."

For too many people, there is no nourishment in these words. Lip-service, yes, but only until it becomes a matter of alternatives: land for the animals, or land for more farms, a dam, an airport, more suburbs, more industrial complexes, more super-highways, more parking lots. People breed cities, and cities breed contempt for the land and the things that grow there naturally.

Let's think selfishly, then. Just as every culture has a folklore, so it has a folk medicine —herbs and leaves and roots prescribed by withered old crones from times forgotten. Some of it is superstition, some of it is nonsense, some of it is outright chicanery, window-dressing for mumbo-jumbo. But some of it is, as they say in television commercials, amazingly effective—and it is certainly time-tested. In fact, many of our modern miracle drugs are derived from, or are synthetic versions of, those very natural substances—herbs, leaves, roots. And of all the hundreds of thousands of plant species growing in the world today that have *not* been tested for their chemical and medicinal properties, isn't it reasonable to assume that there are at least a few that might prove even more miraculous than their predecessors? Wouldn't it be comforting to know that they still existed, waiting to be discovered?

That is a valid reason for saving the plants. But what about animals? What good are they? Listen to Robert Gray again: "We do not need animals as we once did (when we were hunters). But that does not mean that we do not need them at all. . . . There is much we can learn from them that will contribute to our own welfare. Already, many medical discoveries have been made, thanks, in large part, to studies conducted on wild animals. And now, through the relatively new science of ethology—the study of behavior—we are beginning to learn how animals live together in their natural environments. The scientists making these studies think that there could be applications to the way in which we humans might better our own relationships."

Is there anybody who doubts that we humans could use some advice—however indirect and whatever the source—on ways to better our relationships?

There is another selfish reason for saving wild animals, one that may not appeal at first blush to Americans and Europeans, but could prove of inestimable value to the people of the developing lands. When human beings were a hunting species, wild animals were necessary to them as prey. Without wild animals, humans would have remained berry eaters, and their evolution might have taken a dramatically different course. But when they learned to domesticate certain creatures, animals in the wild became a nuisance—predators raided herds and flocks, grain and vegetable eaters got into gardens and fields, grass eaters took food out of the mouths of cattle and sheep. So humans did everything they could to get rid of the competitors wherever their habits and human interests clashed.

Now we are pushing deeper and deeper into the wild lands, and one of our main reasons for doing so is to open up more land for crops and husbandry to feed our surging populations. But much of the land is unsuitable for grains, which keep most of the people in the world alive, or for cattle and sheep. There are vast tracts of semi-arid savannas in Africa, for example, where domestic cattle shrivel and die while several species of wild antelope, adapted to a life of little water and dry grass, grow sleek and fat. With world famine a real threat in the years ahead, would it not make sense to domesticate these antelope—after all, cattle and sheep were wild once—and other animals, too, raising them in areas where they thrive best and little else does, and thereby add to the amount of protein available to avert human starvation?

Pure conservationists may recoil at such a suggestion, but here we are giving selfish reasons for saving wildlife. If the Boer farmers of the 1800s had raised herds of quaggas to feed their slaves, rather than hunting them into extinction, they would have saved for the world a beautiful and useful animal. Admittedly, this sort of conservation by domestication won't help the big cats and other predators, except indirectly, by providing prey for *them,* should any survive. But if the object is to save whatever creatures we can, no method should be scorned.

If there is a "last-ditch" sound to these measures—setting aside patches of habitat where some creatures at least can survive, breeding rare species in captivity in hopes of returning them to their natural environments, if such environments can still be found, and saving others to serve our own selfish ends—it is because we are rapidly approaching a last-ditch situation. We have proved that we are the masters of nature and the tamers of the wilds. And now, while there is still a chance to do so, we must make provisions for other forms of life on the Ark called Earth—before the self-styled first-class passengers take over the entire craft.

Galapagos flightless cormorant
Eric Hosking, F.R.P.S./Bruce Coleman Inc.

NORTH AMERICA
The Wilderness That Was

From the top of Canada and Alaska to the southern tip of Mexico, North America offers a more varied climate and topography than any other land mass except Asia. Across its northern rim, in places penetrating the Arctic Circle, lies a wide belt of treeless tundra, waterlogged in the short northern summer, ice-locked in the long winter. At the bottom, where Mexico's *tierra caliente* tapers and then bulges momentarily before giving way to Guatemala and the other lands of Central America, the climate is tropical and the vegetation so lush that orchids and other air plants grow on the trunks and limbs of trees because they can obtain more light there than on the floor of the forest.

Between these extremes come broad layers of forest, where they still exist—coniferous in the north, deciduous in the middle, mixed below—and a more temperate climate. In the southeast, along the Gulf of Mexico, the coastal plain is fringed with swamps and bayous, and the weather is an introduction to the tropics. In mid-continent, across the mighty Mississippi, corn grows tall on prairies that once nourished towering grasses in which a man on horseback could hide. Farther west, the short-grass, semi-arid plains take over, rising gradually and almost imperceptibly until they reach the wall of the majestic Rocky Mountains. Starting in Alaska, these soaring peaks march southward across Canada and the United States into Mexico, becoming the Sierra Madre on the far side of the Rio Grande. To the west of the mountains, the Great Salt Lake remains as a memory of the vast sea that once covered the area, and jumbled canyons, high plateaus, mesas, and deserts form some of the most spectacular scenery known to man. Another chain of mountains, the Coast Ranges, extending from Alaska to Mexico, marks the Pacific coast of North America. It rises so abruptly from the sea in many areas that there are no coastal plains, but it is a double range, and the valleys in between are among the most fertile in the world.

Western civilization came late to this diverse and bountiful land, but it spread and built with a mindless haste and a waste

unmatched in history. Yet North America still has its wild places, where streams are unpolluted, the air is clear, and people are the intruders. It also has the world's most impressive system of national parks and reserves dedicated to preserving for posterity at least part of the land's natural beauty and native creatures. And its conservation organizations, rising like a stricken conscience from the shocking exploitations of the past, are in the forefront of the battle to protect the earth and its inhabitants from further degradations. It has been truly said that North America is a place where people once did their worst, but are now doing their best, for the environment and the creatures they share it with.

Marty Stouffer

Delmarva Peninsula fox squirrel

The Sea Otter: Saved

Sea otters, smallest of the marine mammals, grow to a length of 4 feet or more and weigh up to 100 pounds. They spend their lives in coastal waters, diving to depths of 120 feet in search of shellfish, and rarely venture on land. One of the most remarkable things about the sea otter is its tool-using ability: floating on its back, it will pound a clam or mussel on a rock on its chest until the shell is broken, then tuck the "anvil" in a loose fold of skin under its forearm, and dive for the next course of its meal.

Sea otters do not have the thick layer of insulating blubber that protects whales and seals from the cold. For warmth and buoyancy they depend upon air trapped in their thick black or brown underfur. Dirt or oil can destroy the fur's insulating capability, so the animal spends long hours every day grooming its coat, for it cannot survive very long if it becomes waterlogged.

At one time the sea otter's pelt was the most valuable fur in the world, so what happened to the animal should come as no surprise. When Georg Wilhelm Steller, the German naturalist, discovered the otters in the Bering Sea in 1741, there were probably at least 100,000 in the population, ranging in a huge arc across the northern Pacific from the Kuriles, north of Japan, around Russia's Kamchatka Peninsula, across the Aleutians to Alaska, and down the coast of North America to Baja California. Then the fur hunters—Russian, Japanese, Chinese, British, and American—went to work with their bloody clubs. By 1840, there were so few otters left that the hunters began to look for other prey. By 1876, the southern race was exterminated off Washington and Oregon. In 1911, the last of the southern sea otters was reported slain near Fort Ord, despite a law passed the year before forbidding the hunting or taking of the animal in American waters. At about the same time an international treaty banning *all* hunting was signed, but the door was being closed on an almost empty barn—the southern race was assumed extinct, and the population of the northern sea otter was down to only about 1,000. Most naturalists believed the animal, a slow reproducer, would shortly become extinct.

Happily, they were wrong. In the favorable habitat of Amchitka Island in the Aleutians, the northern race made a spectacular comeback, reproducing at an unanticipated rate of 10 to 20 percent a year. Today the population numbers about 50,000 and has spread into much of its old range in Alaska, the Aleutians, and Kamchatka.

What of the southern race thought to be extinct? In 1914, a tiny group of 14 was spied off Monterey, California, but for obvious reasons naturalists decided to keep the information secret. Not until 1938, when the population, growing slowly at about 5 percent a year, had reached 100, was the announcement made that the southern sea otter had been "rediscovered." Today there are about 1,000 of the race enjoying life on the California coast, freed of the immediate threat of extinction but restricted in growth by poaching abalone fishermen, who claim the animals raid their catches, and by industrial pollution—"No such animal," says one authority harshly, "can live in a sewer."

Lydekker, *The Royal Natural History*

Endangered Mammals

Indiana bat | *Myotis sodalis*

The total number of living members does not always determine whether or not a species is endangered. There are some 500,000 Indiana bats, but almost all of them winter in three caves and one mine in Kentucky's Carter Caves State Park. To illustrate their vulnerability: one day a few years ago two boys wielding sticks got into one of the caves, and by the time their arms got tired, some 10,000 dead bats littered the floor. Heavy fences and locked gates now protect the insect-eating bats from further mass depredations.

Salt march harvest mouse

Indiana bat

Florida manatee

Mexican grizzly bear | *Ursus horribilis nelsoni*

Southernmost of the grizzlies, the Mexican race is also smaller, but not much—it can reach a length of 6 feet and a weight of almost 700 pounds. It is distinguished from the American black bear by a prominent hump on its shoulders. These grizzlies once ranged from Arizona and New Mexico to Baja California and northern Mexico, but by the 1940s relentless hunting had all but exterminated them. A small group retreated to the hills about fifty miles north of Chihuahua, and game laws were enacted to protect them. Nevertheless, the hunting, trapping, and poisoning continued, and by the 1960s it was believed that the last specimens had been killed. In 1969, however, several were reported on a cattle ranch in Sonora, giving hope that other remnant populations still survive.

Utah prairie dog

Wood bison
Thase Daniel/Bruce Coleman Inc.

30

Mexican grizzly bear

Wood bison | *Bison bison athabascae*

By the late nineteenth century, the millions of
plains and wood bison that had crowded the
West were almost completely destroyed, the
vast numbers reduced to remnants in the
hundreds. About 300 of these were wood
bison, larger and darker than plains bison and
with more slender horns and finer coats. This
herd was located near Great Slave Lake,
where the Canadian government eventually
established Wood Buffalo National Park in
1922. At that time, the herd had increased to
about 2,000. The plains bison had also been
saved, and a few years later more than 6,000
of them were transferred to Wood Buffalo Park
from a crowded reserve in Alberta.
Interbreeding occurred, and the assumption
was that the wood bison had disappeared as a
distinct race. In 1957, however, a pure herd of
200 wood bison was found in a remote section
of the park. Celebration over the discovery was
short-lived, because in the next few years the
race was attacked by various diseases that
caused a serious decline in its numbers.
Control measures were taken, and as an extra
precaution small, independent breeding herds
were moved to other areas of Canada to
ensure the survival of the animal should one
herd be wiped out by disease.

Eastern cougar | *Felis concolor cougar*
Florida cougar | *F. c. coryi*

More than a dozen species and subspecies of
cougars formerly ranged over most of North
America, differing from each other by slight
variations in size and coloring. Basically, all are
sand-colored, with whitish underparts and
black on the ears and muzzle. Also known as
pumas, mountain lions, panthers, and
"painters," the largest reach a length of 8 feet
and a weight of 260 pounds. They are at home
in pine woods, tropical forests, deserts, and
prairies and will attack almost any creature—
including horses, sheep, and cattle—except
humans. In fact, one western race is called
"horse killer." Because of their forays on
human property, these large cats have been
outlawed and slaughtered without mercy. The
Eastern cougar, which once ranged from the
Deep South into Canada and west to the
prairies, was exterminated in the United States
by the beginning of this century but is holding
on tenuously in Canada. The Florida cougar,
formerly common from the Florida keys to the
Carolinas, was considered extinct, but a small
group found sanctuary deep within the Florida
Everglades, and under protection has
increased to between 150 and 300 members.

Cougar

Key deer

Columbian white-tailed deer | *Odocoileus virginianus leucurus*
Key deer | *O. v. clavium*
The white-tailed deer, most widespread deer in America and most hunted big-game animal in the United States, ranges from southern Canada down as far as Brazil and Peru. Some 38 subspecies are recognized, and since their ranges overlap there has been considerable interbreeding. Generally, however, the larger deer are in the north and the smaller in the south. The white tails, snapping erect as a danger signal when the animals are flushed, give them their name. Brought almost to extinction in the United States in the late 1800s, white-tailed deer are now probably more abundant than when the first European colonists arrived, a result of intelligent wildlife management. Two species are in trouble, however. The Columbian white-tailed deer, which once roamed throughout western Washington state and Oregon, has

been reduced to a few hundred animals in the lower part of its range. The Key deer lives only on the Florida keys and has disappeared from many of them, a victim of unrestricted hunting, home construction, and automobiles. By 1949 this smaller, paler version of the mainland white-tail was down to only some 30 individuals. But in 1953 the Key Deer National Wildlife Refuge was established on several of the keys, and the miniature deer is making a "grand comeback"—up to 600 animals in 1973.

Black-footed ferret | *Mustela nigripes*
Probably the rarest mammal in the United States, the black-footed ferret is apparently an innocent victim—a "nontarget species"—of the long war waged by stockmen in the West against prairie dogs. In addition to black feet, this ferret wears a black mask across its eyes and black on the tip of its tail; muzzle, throat, and belly are white, and the rest of the coat is buff. Adults may reach a length of 2 feet, but

weigh only a little over 2 pounds. The ferret's range coincides with that of the prairie dog, from Canada south across the Great Plains to New Mexico, and although not much is known about its habits, it is believed to prey largely on those burrowing rodents. With wide-scale poisoning of prairie dog towns, therefore, the never-abundant black-footed ferret has virtually disappeared from its former haunts, and few sightings have been reported in recent years. Wildlife specialists hope that preservation of prairie dog towns in sanctuaries in the Dakotas will also result in survival of the ferrets.

Northern kit fox | *Vulpes macrotis hebes*
San Joaquin kit fox | *V. m. mutica*
By tradition and legend, foxes are known for their guile. But the kit foxes, of which there once were three species, are not as clever as their relatives. The northern kit fox, once abundant in southern Canada and on the prairies of the Dakotas and Wyoming, reached virtual extinction by the 1920s, succumbing to poison, trapping, and loss of its natural cover. The southern race still survives in the south-

west of the United States, but the San Joaquin kit fox has been reduced to fewer than three thousand members in the dry western valleys of its habitat. In 1960, this fox had some three million suitable acres in which to roam. But irrigation and other forms of land development have shrunk the area, and poisons laid out for rodents, plus illegal hunting, are accelerating the animal's decline. Marked by pointed muzzles, pointed ears, and round, bushy tails, the pale yellowish foxes are graceful and agile—in some areas they're called swift foxes —and are valuable in pest control, since their diet consists of mice, large insects, and gophers, as well as an occasional chicken. Survival of a remnant population may be possible in California's 10,000-acre Kern Animal Refuge.

Florida manatee | *Trichechus manatus latirostris*
Related to whales, dolphins, and porpoises, manatees are large, blimplike creatures with two flippers forward and a fleshy paddle aft. Strictly vegetarian, they browse like cows—

San Joaquin kit fox
Philip Jones

34

they're also called sea cows—in the streams and brackish estuaries of Florida, now their last resort. They may grow as long as 15 feet and weigh a ton. Although they must rank with the homeliest of creatures, legend has it that it was the sight of manatees (and related dugongs) nursing their young at breasts under their flippers that prompted early sailors to start all the talk about mermaids. Seminole Indians once hunted Florida manatees for their hides, oil, and meat, and for a while near the turn of the century a rage for "sea beefsteaks" almost succeeded in wiping out the animal, which ranged then from the Carolinas to the Gulf Coast of Texas. An abortive attempt was made in 1964 to use manatees, which eat as much as a hundred pounds of aquatic plants a day, to help clear Florida's choked streams of water hyacinths, but seven of the eight animals involved in the experiment died, apparently of unseasonal cold, and nothing more was done. Very few manatees are left today, and even though they are protected from hunting they often are brought to grief by the propellers of big power boats. Only 5 were found in a recent head count at the 29,000-acre Chassahowitska Wildlife Refuge near Tampa, and the Florida sea cow may well be on its way to joining Stellar's sea cow, a Pacific relative, which was hunted into extinction in the Bering Sea within three decades of its discovery during the eighteenth century.

Salt marsh harvest mouse | *Reithrodontomys raviventris*
There are sixteen known species of American harvest mice, one of which inhabits salty marshlands. They vary in length from 2 to 5½ inches, and build ball-like nests in tall grass or, sometimes in winter, in burrows. They eat seeds, green shoots, and insects. They do not thrive in cultivated land, and their numbers are dwindling because humans are taking over their habitat. A 3-inch version found in the San Francisco Bay area is in particular trouble from land-fill operations and urban sprawl.

Utah prairie dog | *Cynomys parvidens*
Prairie dogs aren't dogs at all, but a type of ground squirrel—plump, foot-long rodents with flattened heads, coarse brown fur, and a short white tail. Before the coming of the white man, they lived in burrow communities that stretched for miles under the plains, the openings to the burrows marked by mounds of earth, 2 to 4 feet in diameter, carefully piled up and maintained by the animals to prevent surface water from flooding the community. Some years ago, before men set out on a campaign to eradicate prairie dogs, one "city" containing an estimated *400 million* inhabitants was surveyed; it consisted of an intricate system of tunnels under the earth 250 miles long and 100 miles wide! The Utah prairie dog, a species that apparently always has been limited to the state of its name, was never as abundant as others in the family and went into decline about thirty years ago. It can now be found only in a relatively small area of south central Utah, and the fact that its numbers are still diminishing is probably attributable to a recent outbreak of sylvatic plague. It first appeared on the United States endangered list in 1969, was removed in 1970, and put back again in 1973.

Sonoran pronghorn | *Antilocapra americana sonoriensis*
Pronghorn antelopes, blessed with keen sight and hearing and exceptionally fleet of foot, once roamed the semi-arid western plains in herds of millions. Their swiftness was no match for the white hunters' bullets, however, and like the bison, with which they shared their range, they were brought to the edge of extinction in the nineteenth century. Again like the bison, they were saved by conservation laws, and have made a spectacular recovery—all except the Sonoran race. This southern antelope, down to a few individuals in Arizona and probably no more than a thousand in Mexico, may not survive without cooperation between United States and Mexican authorities.

Volcano rabbit | *Romerolagus fiazi*
Existing only on hillside slopes covering an area of ten by twenty miles in the Valley of Mexico, a few miles east of Mexico City, the volcano rabbit (named for the volcanic soil in the valley) has the most restricted range of any Mexican mammal. Called *teporingo* by

Mexicans, it is distinguished by short ears, the lack of a tail, short legs and feet, and a high-pitched voice that it uses often—the world's only talking rabbit. In its open pine environment it feeds on coarse grasses called *zacaton* and a type of aromatic mint. The grasses also provide cover for its underground burrows, and recent encroachments by farmers, who burn off the grass to make room for crops, is severely narrowing the rabbit's already limited habitat. Hunters from Mexico City are also contributing to the decline of the volcano rabbit, shooting it not to eat but for target practice or to feed their dogs.

Philip Jones

Volcano rabbit

Morro Bay kangaroo rat | *Dipodomys heermanni morroensis*
Kangaroo rats look—and hop—just like miniature kangaroos, only 7 inches long with a tail of equal length. They leave their burrows at night to feed on seeds, buds, and leaves, carrying the booty back to the nest in their cheek pouches. There are some twenty species ranging across the Southwest and into Mexico. One, the Morro Bay kangaroo rat, is being pressured in its California range by human activity and is now under state and federal protection.

Delmarva Peninsula fox squirrel | *Sciurus niger cinereus*

This grayish squirrel, whose bushy tail displays a prominent black stripe, formerly ranged through a good part of Delaware, Maryland, and Pennsylvania, but is now limited to a few counties on Maryland's Eastern Shore. Probably only a few thousand have survived the steady deterioration of their habitat as forests give way to farms and towns. Their hope now rests in the establishment of protected forest areas—especially stands of loblolly pine —as in the Pocomoke State Forest.

Lydekker, *The Royal Natural History*

Morro Bay kangaroo rat

36

American Museum of Natural History

Kaibab squirrel

Kaibab squirrel | *Sciurus kaibabensis*

The condition of this dark gray squirrel, touched with reddish brown on its back, black tufts on its ears, and a bushy white tail, illustrates some of the difficulties inherent in describing a species as "endangered." It inhabits the Kaibab Plateau, located in Arizona near the Grand Canyon, where it is said to feed almost exclusively on the cambium layer of yellow pines. For many years it has been protected by law, yet for incompletely understood reasons its population fluctuates. Numbers reached a peak some thirty years ago, but now are down to about 1,000 individuals, the lowest point in more than fifty years. The federal government has included the squirrel on its endangered list, but Arizona wildlife officials disagree, contending that the present population is about all the remaining habitat can support.

Beach meadow vole | *Microtus breweri*
Block Island meadow vole | *M. pennsylvanicus provectus*

Voles, sometimes called meadow mice, are extremely prolific. Each female, after becoming sexually mature at the age of two months, can produce up to 100 young a year in litter after litter. Despite this fecundity, the Block Island meadow vole is in trouble, because it is limited to one island off the New England coast, where intensive construction has denuded its natural grassy habitat. The beach meadow vole has a similar problem. Once abundant along the North Atlantic coast up to Newfoundland, it is now restricted to Muskegat Island, six miles west of Nantucket, where it survives under harsh climate conditions, including hurricanes and violent storms that erode its nesting sites. Household cats gone wild, plus the expansion of human activities, also pose a threat.

Establishment of a refuge on the island for nesting terns will help the vole, but the cats may still have the last word unless they are removed from Muskegat.

Red wolf | *Canis rufus*

The red wolf, long of leg, big of ear, and large of body, but as often gray or tawny as red, once ranged through Texas and Oklahoma up to Illinois and Indiana, and eastward through the Carolinas. Like the gray wolf, it prefers forests and thickets, and conversion of woodlands into farmland has destroyed much of its habitat. But human fear and hatred, leading to attempts at total eradication, probably have contributed even more to the animal's decline. Positive identification of red wolves is difficult because of widespread interbreeding with coyotes. The only known population of pure red wolves survives in a marshy area along the Texas Gulf Coast and perhaps extends into Louisiana. Here live an estimated three hundred animals, and here the United States Office of Endangered Species has been making its first attempt to bring back a species. The hybrids are invading the area, however, and unless they can be stopped officials fear that the red wolves in this last pocket may breed themselves out of existence.

Eastern timber wolf | *Canis lupus lycaon*
Northern Rocky Mountain wolf | *C. l. irremotus*

In 1630, Massachusetts put a penny-a-pelt bounty on the wolf; other colonies followed suit, and by the time of the American Revolution, wolves were almost extinct in New England and parts of Canada. Young men went west, taking their hatred of wolves with them, and today there are only a few pockets of these important predators left in the United States—the Northern Rocky Mountain wolf in the remote regions of its range, and the Eastern timber wolf, which once ranged most of the continent, now down to an estimated seven thousand, most of them in Alaska, Canada, and Superior National Forest in Minnesota. A campaign is under way to prove to fearful people that the wolf is not at all as ferocious as painted in legend, but on the contrary is a

helpful natural force in maintaining the health of the herds of game animals on which it preys. Early in 1974, four wolves trapped by the United States Bureau of Fish and Wildlife in Minnesota were released in Michigan in an attempt

Marty Stouffer

Red wolf

to revive the species there. Also good news for the wolf was a decision by the United States Department of Defense—made under extreme pressure—to use synthetic fibers for the linings of 277,502 Army parka hoods instead of the originally specified wolf fur. If the initial design had been carried out, it is estimated that at least half the surviving timber wolves—already on the government's endangered list—would have been sacrificed.

Endangered Birds

Masked bobwhite | *Colinus virginianus ridgwayi*

Similar to the common bobwhite of the eastern United States but slightly smaller, the male masked bobwhite has a deep red breast, black head and throat, and a line of white forming the "mask" over its eyes. It formerly ranged in southern Arizona and Sonora, Mexico, traveling in coveys of 15 or 20 so closely formed that hunters often brought down half the group with one blast of buckshot. Cattle, however, rather than hunters, are the main reason for the bird's decline, for they crop the tall grass the bobwhite needs for nesting and protection. The birds disappeared from Arizona at about the turn of the century, and have been reintroduced several times, so far unsuccessfully, with captive stock bred at research centers. An estimated one thousand birds survive in the wild in Sonora.

Attwater's greater prairie chicken | *Tympanuchus cupido attwateri*
Greater prairie chicken | *T. c. pinnatus*
Lesser prairie chicken | *T. c. pallidicinctus*

There once were four subspecies of prairie chickens. Now the heath hen, which ranged through New England and the Mid-Atlantic states, is gone. Attwater's, the southern race that was distributed from southwestern Louisiana across Texas to northern Mexico, was down to 2,200 birds in 1971 and only 1,650 a year later. The greater prairie chicken of the Midwest and the lesser prairie chicken of the Southwest are vulnerable, and their numbers are decreasing over much of their range. In all cases their plight is the same: as the tall grass country falls under the plow or the grazing of cattle and sheep, the birds have nowhere to go. Land has been acquired for managed habitats in a number of states, and more is being sought to prevent the extermination not just of a single species, but of an entire genus.

Mississippi sandhill crane | *Grus canadensis pulla*

Of all the subspecies of sandhill cranes—large

Masked bobwhite

Mississippi sandhill crane

40

Attwater's greater prairie chicken

birds that have survived relatively unchanged since the Lower Pliocene age of nine million years ago—the dark-plumaged Mississippi crane is in the most trouble. Restricted in its range—the Gulf coastal plain of Louisiana, Mississippi, and Alabama—it is nearing extinction as suburban development and drainage of wetlands reduce its habitat. Probably no more than 30 to 40 birds are left, centering in Jackson County, Mississippi, plus a dozen or so more being reared in captivity from eggs taken from nests in the wild.

Whooping crane | *Grus americana*

In the early nineteenth century, observers at a given time would report so many whoopers flying by on their annual migration that hours passed before the sky was clear. Yet, in 1945, only 17 birds were known for certain to exist, and the species seemed doomed. A large, spectacular white bird with black wing-tips and black on its head, the whooper roamed over most of North America in Pleistocene times. Today, the few that survive in the wild—51 counted in 1972—breed only in Wood Buffalo National Park in Canada and winter on the Aransas National Wildlife Refuge in Texas. Although some birds are lost each year on the 2,500-mile migration, usually because of illegal hunting or flying into power lines, stringent protection has brought their numbers creeping back up. Zoologists have succeeded in raising whooping cranes in captivity from eggs taken from nests in the wild—one egg out of a clutch of two is removed without affecting the production of the wild birds, since the parent cranes rarely rear more than one young. In a recent count there were about two dozen captive birds, most of them at the Patuxent Wildlife Research Center in Maryland, where they are being raised as breeding stock to replenish the crane in the wild.

Eskimo curlew | *Numenius borealis*

Also known as *pi-pi-pi-uk* or *tura-tura* by the Eskimos, and by others as prairie pigeon, fute, chittering curlew, and doughbird (because it is so fat in the summer), the Eskimo curlew may have more popular names than surviving individuals. If these buff-colored birds with a slightly curved, 2-inch-long bill had elected to stay in their breeding grounds in the Canadian North and Alaska, they probably would be in good shape today. But each year they made the 8,000-mile migratory flight to their winter quarters in South America, and their flyways were lined, both going and coming, with eager hunters armed with shotguns. Before the end of the nineteenth century, the huge flocks had disappeared, wiped out by overhunting. The bird has long been considered extinct, but a total of 8 sightings of 1 or 2 migrants in the last quarter century offer at least a scant hope that it still survives. Zoologists now hope to find its

Eskimo curlew

New York Public Library

Southern bald eagle

California Condor: Future Uncertain

The California condor hangs on, a Pleistocene relic whose 9-foot wingspan casts a shadow on the conscience of modern man. Save-the-condor groups have proliferated in the West, making the fate of this great ugly bird, the largest soaring land bird in North America, the symbol of their desire for an environment capable of sustaining all forms of life. There is a touch of irony in the fact that this huge eater of carrion, with roots in the primitive ages of the world, should have an effect on the construction of dams and superhighways, the flight patterns of airlines and the drilling of oil fields.

Yet the future is bleak for the condor. Only 50 or 60 birds survive, despite protective laws and the establishment of breeding refuges. Part of the problem is loss of birds through hunting—illegal or accidental. Poison takes its share, too—the condors eat bait laced with strychnine intended for coyotes and other "vermin," or make a deadly feast of creatures that died from eating the poisoned bait. Real estate developers and citrus growers are slowly but surely crowding them out of parts of their habitat, and the dwindling of antelope and mule deer herds, plus the conversion of rangeland to crops, reduces their food supply. This latter threat may affect their rate of reproduction, already low at one hatchling every other year. And if a creature cannot bring its birth rate at least to a level with its death rate, there is no way for it to step back from the brink on which it teeters.

breeding and wintering sites to determine what factors might be limiting its ability to increase.

Mexican duck | *Anas diazi*

A large bird, the Mexican duck is losing ground because of disappearing wetlands in the southwestern United States and northern Mexico, where it ranges. Despite a population of some 15,000 in Mexico and about 500 north of the border, it is considered extremely vulnerable, in part because of increasing hybridization with the common mallard—perhaps, say some sources, because the changing habitat is more suitable to mallards. Restocking of former breeding areas has begun with captive birds, and efforts are being made to establish reserves with suitable habitat.

Southern bald eagle | *Haliaeetus leucocephalus leucocephalus*

About 15,000 bald eagles, symbol of the United States, still survive in the wild, but most of them belong to the northern race and can be found primarily in Alaska. The southern race, ranging from New Jersey south to Florida and west to southern California, has been brought to a status of near extinction by a combination of habitat loss, illegal shooting, and pesticides. Only a few hundred active nests have been counted, the largest concentration, about fifty pairs, in the Everglades National Park. The ban by the United States on the widespread use of DDT should help the eagles, and extensive efforts are being made by govern-ment bodies and such organizations as the Audubon Society to save the bird. Landowners of more than three million acres in Florida have agreed to treat nesting areas as bald eagle sanctuaries, and access to nesting areas in all national wildlife refuges is severely restricted.

American peregrine falcon | *Falco peregrinus anatum*
Arctic peregrine falcon | *F. p. tundrius*
Prairie falcon | *F. mexicanus*

One of the earliest victims of thinning egg shells caused by the cumulative effects of chlorinated pesticides, the American peregrine falcon, a medium-sized hawk with long, pointed wings and a long tail, has been

Jeff Foott/Bruce Coleman Inc.

Prairie falcon

exterminated east of the Rockies in the United States and in most of eastern Canada during the past twenty years. It is now in serious trouble elsewhere, even in the remote regions of northern Canada and Alaska. The Arctic peregrine, similar in appearance but smaller and paler, is following the same grim pattern. The number of birds breeding and the number of successful hatchings both are decreasing drastically. Estimates put from 200 to 300 pairs of birds in Arctic Alaska, and perhaps several thousand in Arctic Canada; no estimates of birds in Greenland, the other breeding range, are available. All falcons are protected, but since they seem to be so vulnerable to chemi-cal poisoning, such protection may become moot unless food chain pesticides are elimi-nated from the environment. The prairie falcon of the West has also disappeared from many areas of its range in Canada and the United States, and although data available is still inadequate, it seems reasonable to assume this bird is falling victim to the same factors causing the decline of the other falcons.

southeastern Mexico, usually in humid mountain forests. Deforestation, hunting, and volcanic action all have contributed to its decline. Mexican law now forbids hunting the horned guan, but conservationists in the country are not optimistic about the bird's long-range prospects for survival unless sanctuaries can be established and controlled there and in Guatemala.

Florida Everglade kite | *Rostrhamus sociabilis plumbeus*
Also called snail kite because apple snails apparently are the only food it eats, the Florida Everglade kite is the northernmost of four species of kites inhabiting the Americas. The male is slate gray with a black head and wingtips, light gray on the tailtip, and has red legs and eyes; the female has a white tail patch, white over the eyes, and a buff body streaked with dark lines. Both sexes have the heavily curved, sharp bill that kites have developed for getting at their snail prey. Found only in Florida and already in trouble from the guns of duck hunters, the Everglade kite rapidly declined with the draining of marshes in the

Aleutian Canada goose | *Branta canadensis leucopareia*
This small brown and gray goose with a broad white band at the base of its black neck once nested on many of the Aleutian Islands and migrated to California and Japan. Then Arctic foxes were introduced on the islands intentionally—by men who sell furs—and rats by accident. Both predators preyed on the ground-nesting geese, and now there are only 250 to 300 birds left, limited to nesting on Buldir Island, so inaccessible that neither foxes nor rats ever got there. The foxes have been removed from two of the other islands, and the progeny of captive birds reared at the Patuxent Wildlife Research Center in Maryland have been released there in a first effort to reestablish the Aleutian Canada goose in its former breeding range.

Horned guan | *Oreophasis derbianus*
A large, handsome, tree-living bird with powerful, prehensile feet, the horned guan is found in southwestern Guatemala and

American Museum of Natural History

Florida Everglade kite

45

state. It is known now only in the Lake Okeechobee area and in the northern Everglades, and numbered only about 120 in 1969. Establishment of sanctuaries, plus control of water-based weeds to aid the propagation of apple snails, might save the kite from extinction.

California brown pelican | *Pelecanus occidentalis californicus*
Eastern brown pelican | *P. o. carolinensis*
Both of these large water birds have been much reduced from their former numbers by the pesticide-induced problem of thin shells. The Eastern pelican, which formerly ranged the Atlantic coast from North Carolina down to South America and along the Gulf Coast, is now down to 8,500 breeding pairs in the United States, most of them in Florida. There are no available estimates of numbers living in South and Central America, but evidence of thinning egg shells has turned up in Panama. The larger California brown pelican breeds along the California coast and down into Mexico. The population is estimated to be about 100,000, but is declining in California at a rate of 14 to 18 percent a year.

Clapper rail

California clapper rail | *Rallus longirostris*
Light-footed clapper rail | *R. l. levipes*
Yuma clapper rail | *R. l. yumanensis*
Like the prairie chickens, these three rails are suffering from loss of habitat—in their case, salt marshes and wetlands. The California rail is declining as the salt marshes of San Francisco Bay and along the coast become polluted, affecting its food supply, or are drained and filled for urban development. Similar factors are reducing the light-footed rails in southern California, where survivors may number only in the low hundreds. The Yuma rail, resident of the marshes of the lower Colorado River and the southeastern end of the Salton Sea, is being affected not only by marsh drainage and removal of marsh plants, but by increasing salinity of the Salton Sea.

Cape Sable sparrow | *Ammospiza mirabilis*
A few scattered populations of this tiny, olive gray sparrow live in fresh and brackish marshes of southwestern Florida. Real estate

Eastern brown pelican

The Trumpeter Swan: Saved

In the early 1930s there were only 60 or so trumpeter swans left in the United States outside Alaska, with perhaps 40 more in western Canada. The reasons for the decline of the magnificent bird, the largest swan of North America, are familiar: overhunting and the demands of the feather trade, combined with the spread of farming into the trumpeter's wetland habitat.

Things looked bad, but then, in 1935, the Red Rock Lakes Migratory Waterfowl Refuge was established in southwestern Montana, and the fortunes of the great bird took a marked turn for the better. Totaling more than 40,000 acres, much of it historic breeding grounds for the swans, the refuge started with fewer than 50 birds. Within three years the population had doubled to 98, and by 1944 it had jumped to 207. The figure stood at 417 in 1951, and since then the population has stabilized with about 500 birds producing 100 cygnets a year.

Dr. E. R. Degginger, APSA

Transferring stock from Red Rock Lakes to other reserves in Oregon, Nevada, South Dakota, Wyoming, and Manitoba has worked well, and today the world population of trumpeter swans is well over 2,000—one of the brightest pages in the history of animal conservation, and convincing proof that wise wildlife management can in many cases turn what appeared to be impending doom into a cause for celebration.

development and such natural hazards as hurricanes and fire are taking away their habitat, and there may be fewer than 500 left.

Dusky seaside sparrow | *Ammospiza nigrescens*
Part of the remaining population of this blackish sparrow of Florida's coastal marshes is in Merritt Island National Wildlife Refuge. Elsewhere on the island, and along the mainland coast where most of the birds live, draining of marshes and impoundments for mosquito control are shrinking an already limited habitat. In 1969, there were an estimated 1,000 to 2,000 birds. Now there may be fewer than 500.

Ipswich sparrow | *Passerculus princeps*
These streaked, sandy-colored birds breed only on Sable Island, off Nova Scotia, and winter among the costal sand dunes south to Georgia. They are in decline because erosion of tiny Sable Island is reducing their available

breeding area, and because residential development is taking over their wintering beaches. Setting aside additional wildlife refuges with undisturbed sand dunes in coastal areas may save them.

California least tern | *Sterna albifrons browni*
This small white tern, black capped and with a pale gray mantle, nests on beaches along the coast of California. Because of human intrusion on the beaches, along with motor scooters and dune buggies, the bird is disappearing, although some have nested on new land made of dredged sand south of Los Angeles. In 1970, active nesting sites were down to 15 and nesting pairs down to 300.

Bachman's warbler | *Vermivora bachmanii*
Considered the rarest native songbird, this tiny green, yellow, and black warbler may have been on its way to extinction when it was discovered in South Carolina by John Bachman. Individuals and small groups were

spotted infrequently over the years in the area between Missouri and the Carolinas, but the last group of any size was recorded in 1889, when 21 birds of a flock migrating to Cuba were killed when they struck a lighthouse beacon in Florida. No one knows how many are left, defying extinction in the still extensive swampy river forests of the southeastern United States.

Golden-cheeked warbler | *Dendroica chrysoparia*

A dark little bird with bright yellow cheeks, this warbler breeds primarily in stands of mature juniper trees, twenty-five to forty feet tall, on Edward's Plateau in central Texas, and winters in Central America. The total population is about 14,000 birds, and the species would not be considered endangered except for the fact that its habitat is extremely specialized and limited—and the common agricultural practice in Texas is to clear out trees to create more grassland. A mark of our growing conservation maturity may be seen in a recent court ruling that prevented developers from converting one breeding area of the golden-cheeked warbler into a golf course.

Kirtland's warbler | *Dendroica kirtlandii*

This small, bluish gray bird with black streaks on its back breeds only among young jack pines with bushy undergrowth on Michigan's Lower Peninsula, and winters only in the Bahamas. It is vulnerable because of its limited range, exact breeding habitat requirements, increasing parasitism by cowbirds, and its small numbers—probably no more than 300 pairs. Private and government agencies are cooperating in setting aside areas where controlled burning will provide a succession of young stands of jack pine for nesting sites, and attempts are being made to obtain protection of the bird's wintering sites in the Bahamas.

Imperial woodpecker | *Campephilus imperialis*

Worthy of its name because it is the largest woodpecker in the world, the imperial once ranged throughout the mountain pine-oak forests of the Sierra Madre in northern Mexico.

Lumbering in the mountains is responsible for the collapse of the bird's population during the last half century, but in an indirect way. The lumbering operation is selective, leaving many large trees standing. But the men doing the cutting are not selective in the birds they shoot for sport or pot, and a large, colorful bird like the imperial woodpecker is an irresistible target. Since 1960, the bird has been recorded in only two localities, and in one, the upland forests of Durango, it seems subsequently to have disappeared.

Cactus Clyde Productions

Bachman's warbler

Ivory-billed woodpecker | *Campephilus principalis*

Extinct—but maybe not quite. That's the best that can be said about this large, showy woodpecker, bigger than a crow, distinguished by its white bill, large white patches on its wings, and a crest red in the male and black in the female. It was formerly resident in the southeastern United States, where it lived in aging forests, feeding on beetles that infest dead and dying trees. As the whine of the logging crews advanced through the forests, the tin-horn call of the ivory-billed woodpecker receded, and it is heard no more over the bird's former range. Occasional sightings, mostly unconfirmed, in Louisiana, Texas, and South Carolina, suggest that perhaps half a dozen birds survive, and wildlife experts hope that establishment of overripe forest reserves might yet save them. A related race, the Cuban ivory-bill (*C. p. bairdi*) has undergone a similar decline in Cuba as the forests dwindled, and as long ago as 1956 there were only a dozen birds to be counted.

Red-cockaded woodpecker | *Dendrocopus borealis*

Good forestry management includes the removal of old, diseased trees, but abandonment of this practice in some of the pine woodlands in the southeast by the United States Forest Service and several timber companies has given new hope to the red-cockaded woodpecker. This small bird, which shows black and white stripes on its back, white cheeks and underparts, and, in the male, a small red spot on each side of the black cap, nests only in living pines infected with red-heart disease. The bird is still vulnerable, because the number of these specialized nesting sites is limited, but estimated numbers now range from 3,000 to 10,000.

Cactus Clyde Productions

Red-cockaded woodpecker

Endangered Fishes

Humpback chub | *Gila cypha*
Little is known about this small-mouthed, small-eyed fish, but it occurs in such small numbers in widely separated places in the Green and Colorado rivers that it is considered in jeopardy. Research is under way to obtain more information.

Longjaw cisco | *Coregonus alpenae*
An important commercial chub fish in Lakes Michigan and Huron until the 1950s, this medium-size cisco is now severely depleted. Reasons include intensive commercial fishing, increased competition from other fish, and predation from sea lampreys. In Lake Erie, pollution has reduced the population to a very low number. No protective measures have been taken. Two other ciscoes, the blackfin and the deepwater, are almost certainly extinct.

Cui-ui | *Chasmistes cujus*
Large and heavy-bodied, this six-pound sucker is a relict species of a genus of three lake suckers, and is considered to have the best chance for survival. Formerly more widespread in Nevada, it is now limited to Pyramid Lake. Its decline elsewhere was brought about primarily by a reduced flow in the Truckee River because of dam construction and irrigation. The fish is of economic importance to the Indians in the area and of biological importance to science. Catch limits have been imposed on non-Indians, and efforts are being made to restock in Pyramid and other suitable lakes.

Blue pike | *Stizostedionvitreum glaucum*
The color of its name, the blue pike contributed more than 20 million pounds a year to the catch of Lake Erie commercial fishermen and 500,000 pounds to the Lake Ontario industry before its swift decline in the mid-1950s. It has now almost disappeared in both lakes, a victim of modern-day pollution and environment destruction. In 1969, when the situation was recognized as desperate, a pair of fish was spawned at a Pennsylvania fish station and 9,000 fry were transferred to a national fish hatchery in South Dakota. Later, some of the fingerlings were stocked in an isolated lake in Minnesota, the start of a campaign to save this valuable fish.

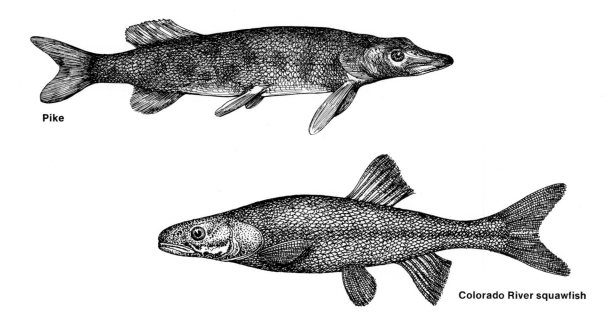

Pike

Colorado River squawfish

Philip Jones

50

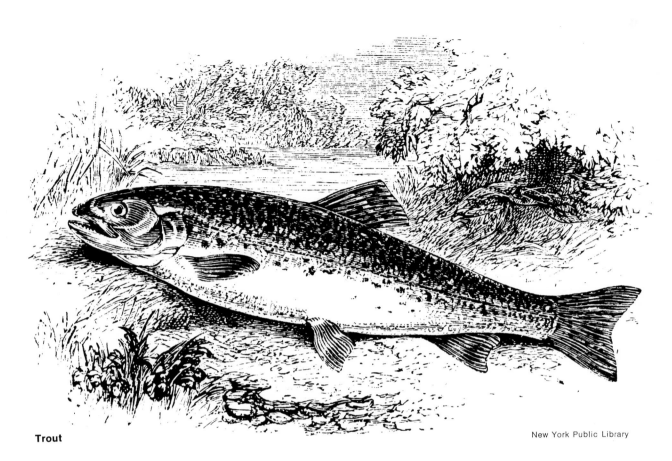

Trout

Colorado squawfish | *Ptychocheilus lucius*
Long and slender, with a dusky green back
and silvery sides, this fish that once was widely
distributed throughout the Colorado River and
its tributaries is now limited to parts of the Salt
River, the middle and lower section of the
Green River, and the upper reaches of the
Colorado. It is adapted to life in swift, warm
rivers and will not reproduce in the cold
tailwaters or reservoirs behind high dams.

Shortnose sturgeon | *Acipenser brevirostrum*
A small sturgeon rarely more than 3 feet
long, this fish formerly lived in Atlantic seaboard
rivers from New Brunswick to Florida. It has
now disappeared from most of its range, with
pollution the probable major cause and
overfishing a contributing factor. All recent
records are from the Hudson River, with the
exception of one specimen taken in Florida.
No protective measures have been adopted yet.

Arizona trout | *Salmo sp.*
Somewhat similar to the Gila trout, the
Arizona, or Apache, trout is now restricted to
two small streams and two small lakes in
Arizona. Several thousand fish are held at the
Arizona State hatchery for restocking.

Gila trout | *Salmo gilae*
Once widespread in the upper tributaries
of the Gila and San Francisco rivers in New
Mexico, this golden yellow trout is now limited
to a few creeks in Gila National Forest.
Elsewhere, the loss of forest damaged its
habitat, and competition from introduced fish
proved overpowering.

Greenback cutthroat trout | *Salmo clarki
stomias*
Weighing less than a pound, this small
trout—the original cutthroat in streams
feeding the South Platte River in Colorado—

51

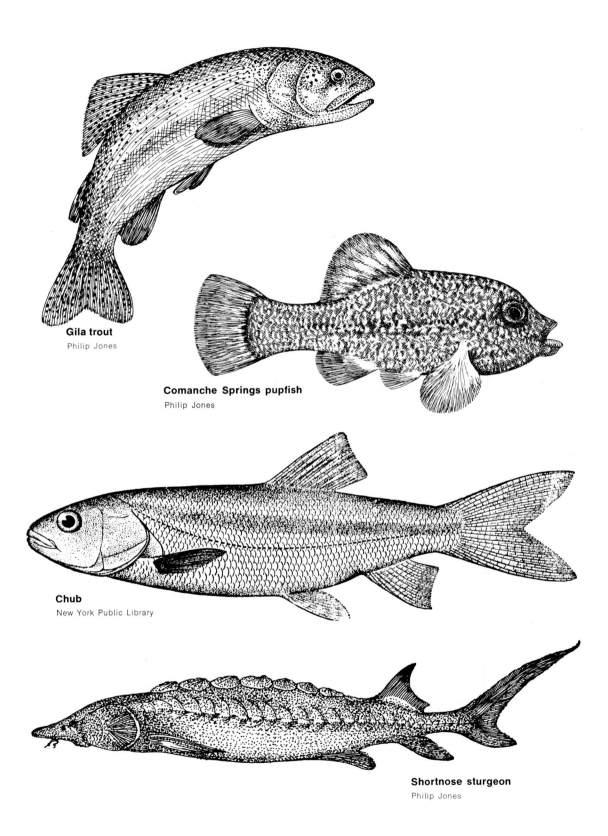

Gila trout

Philip Jones

Comanche Springs pupfish

Philip Jones

Chub

New York Public Library

Shortnose sturgeon

Philip Jones

was down to only an estimated 10 pure specimens in 1968. Competition from larger stocked trout, hybridization, and damage to streams by human activities probably all contributed to its decline. Reclamation and restocking of suitable waters, together with restrictions on fishing and barriers to keep other trout out, might bring this fish back.

Lahontan cutthroat trout | *Salmo clarki henshawi*

This large 10- to 15-pound sport fish is adapted to highly alkaline lakes in the Lahontan Basin in California and Nevada. In some lakes it is extinct. In others, a total of about 4,000 survive in pure populations, plus some hybrids. Reasons for its decline are diverse: damage to spawning beds caused by lumbering, overgrazing, and fires; diversion of water for irrigation; pollution; dam-blocked spawning runs; competition from introduced trout; and hybridization. Other trout are no longer stocked in the lakes, and the Lahontan National Fish Hatchery has been established to breed this fish back to reasonable numbers.

Paiute cutthroat trout | *Salmo clarki seleniris*

Only about 500 adults of this colorful orange-red and white trout survive in several creeks in and near Yosemite National Park in California. Their limited range has worked against them, and overfishing and hybridization with rainbow trout have helped to bring the numbers of pure-breds in the population down. A few transplants of pure stock have been made, and a number of creeks have been closed to fishing.

Other endangered fish

The following fish, most of them quite small and most of them residents of the West, are lumped together because they have at least one thing in common: all are confined to such limited areas that their status is highly vulnerable. Many of them are threatened by the same conditions, and in some cases a combination of conditions: silting from road construction and deforestation, dam construction, industrial pollution, human tampering with their habitat, introduction of predator and competitor exotics, removal of vegetation, drainage and irrigation projects, and their own restricted numbers. In many cases remedial measures are under way, but not all may be successful.

The list includes the Pahranagat bonytail (*Gila robusta jordani*); Mohave chub (*G. [Siphateles] mohavensis*); Kendall Warm Springs dace (*Rhinichthys osculus thermalis*); Moapa dace (*Moapa coriacea*); the Fountain, Maryland, Okaloosa, and Watercress darters (*Etheostoma fonticola, E. sellare, E. okaloosae*, and *E. nuchale*); the Big Bend, Clear Creek, and Pecos gambusias (*Gambusia gaigei, G. heterochir,* and *G. noblis*); Pahrump killifish (*Empetrichthys latos*); Comanche Springs, Devils Hole, Owens River, Tecopa, and Warm Spring pupfish (*Cyprinodon elegans, C. diabolis, C. radiosus, C. nevadensis claidae,* and *C. nevadensis pectoralis*); Unarmored threespine stickleback (*Gasterosteus aculeatus williamsoni*); Gila topminnow (*Poeciliopsis occidentalis occidentalis*); and the Woundfin (*Plagopherus argentissimus*).

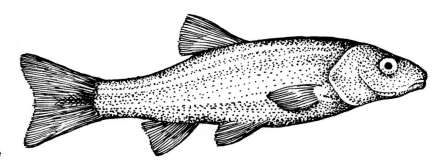

Moapa dace
Philip Jones

Endangered Reptiles and Amphibians

American alligator | *Alligator mississippiensis*

Resident of the swamps, rivers, and lakes of the southeastern United States, the American alligator has been hunted unmercifully for its hide, especially the softer skin from the underside. For this reason, the 19- and 20-foot giants of the past are seen no more, and even 10-foot specimens are rare. Although alligators may once have had worldwide distribution, there are only two widely separated species left, the American, and the Chinese alligator, which is found only in China's upper Yangtze River valley. Females of the American form lay 20 to 50 eggs in a nest of mud and vegetable matter, and after about 10 weeks of natural incubation come back at the sound of peeping to tear open the nest and release the young, each of which is about 8 inches long and brightly colored in black and yellow. It has been estimated that the American alligator's numbers have been reduced by 98 percent since 1960 because of illegal hunting. Protective state and federal laws have resulted in some recovery in local areas, giving rise to a hope that alligator "farms" could be established and the animal removed from the endangered list. But widespread poaching has continued, and unless it can be stopped, experts consider the outlook for the embattled alligator bleak.

Philip Jones

Blunt-nosed leopard lizard

Blunt-nosed leopard lizard | *Crotaphytus silus*

This yellowish brown lizard, long and slender, is covered with black or brown splotches that surround numerous red dots. It is identical to the related leopard lizard except for its shorter snout. Limited to California's San Joaquin Valley and parts of Washington State, it had reached, experts believed, "the verge of total extinction" as its grassland habitat was converted to agricultural use. A later study put the population at 100 per square mile, but as more of the valley is opened up to farming, the earlier estimate may prove to be the true one.

Desert slender salamander | *Batrachoseps aridus*

It is unknown whether or not this small, slender land salamander is in decline, for it came to the attention of science so recently

American alligator

John Tveten

that there is no information about possible former distribution. It is known to exist now in a population estimated at fewer than 500, in Hidden Palm Canyon in California's Santa Rosa Mountains. These salamanders can be found under limestone sheeting on the canyon walls during the summer and under rock talus the rest of the year. This limited habitat makes them particularly vulnerable, for destruction of the limestone sheeting would probably result in extinction for these salamanders.

Santa Cruz long-toed salamander |
Ambystoma macrodactylum croceum
Known to exist only at two localities in California: Valencia Lagoon, near Aptos in Santa Cruz County, and Ellicott Pond, four miles west of Watsonville. At Valencia Lagoon, this salamander was almost eradicated when road builders putting in a four-lane highway drained the pond in which the animals live and breed. A temporary pond hurriedly dammed up saved the salamanders, and California is now trying to restore the original habitat. The other population, at Ellicott Pond, is threatened by a proposed trailer park. The very rarity of these black and gold amphibians has caused both professional and amateur biologists to hunt them assiduously, thereby adding to the problem of survival.

Texas blind salamander | *Typhlomolge rathbuni*
There is some question about the status of this amphibian, formerly found in artesian wells, underground streams, and caves in Hays County, Texas. Few specimens have been seen in recent years as a result of well capping, heavy drainage of underground streams, and overcollecting by amateur biologists and dealers in rare animals. But, says one zoologist, there may be unexplored caverns under the earth housing large populations. Similar to the blind white salamander of Europe, this species appears pink because its skin lacks pigment, allowing the blood in its veins to show through.

San Francisco garter snake | *Thamnophis sirtalis tetrataenia*
Striped in yellow, red, and black, with red

on the top of its head, this harmless snake ranks with the most vividly colored American serpents. It is losing its marshy habitat in the San Francisco area to urban developers and highway construction crews, and only a few hundred remain in scattered colonies around reservoirs serving the region. California biologists are breeding adults and releasing the young in their native areas.

Houston toad | *Bufo houstonensis*
This small toad is considered practically extinct, a result of the destruction of its habitat in south-central Texas. It is now known from only a few localities, with populations counted in the dozens, and is most numerous in Bastrop and Buescher State Parks. The growth of the city of Houston, plus the destruction of stands of loblolly pine through lumbering and road construction, have led to loss of habitat. Also contributing to the decline of the Houston toad is hybridization with two other more numerous species.

Atlantic ridley turtle | *Lepidochelys kempi*
The ridleys are the smallest of the sea turtles, attaining a length of only about 27 inches. The Atlantic, or Kemp's, ridley has 5 pairs of costal scutes—horny plates—with minute pores on their hind borders, and a snout covered by 2 pairs of prefrontal shields. At one time the ridleys were thought, mistakenly, to be a hybrid between loggerheads and hawksbills or green turtles. The only known breeding beaches of this rare turtle are on the Gulf Coast of northern Mexico, although individuals have been recorded nesting in Texas and farther south, in Mexico. During the nesting, or *arribada,* which may occur 3 times a year at different beaches in the breeding ground, hundreds and sometimes thousands of females used to come ashore to lay their eggs. At one *arribada* years ago, an estimated 40,000 turtles filled the beach. But those days seem to be over, brought to a close by egg-poaching men who not only clean out the nests but capture the females on their way to the nesting site and crack them open to get at the eggs. Mexico now protects the ridley, and if poaching can be controlled the turtle may make a comeback.

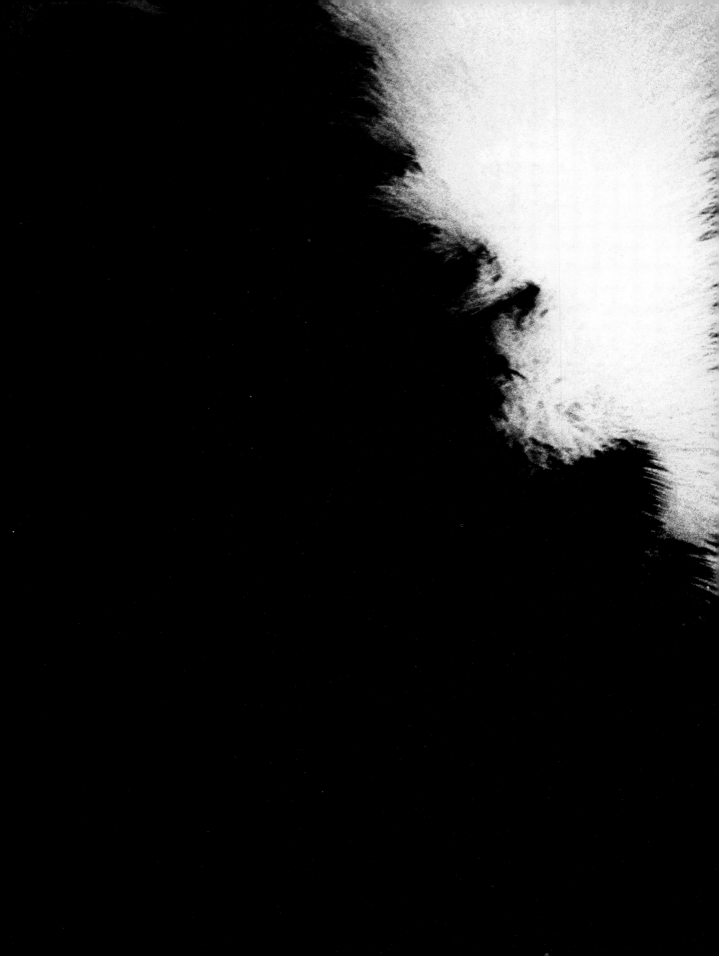

CENTRAL AND SOUTH AMERICA
Nature's Last Stand

Three things dominate South America and turn it into a land of superlatives. The first, the magnificent range of the Andes, rises from the toe of Chile and hugs the Pacific coast for more than 4,500 miles, like the backbone of a gigantic prehistoric creature. The longest mountain chain in the world, it sends more than fifty snow-capped peaks soaring 20,000 or more feet into the air and grudgingly offers passes at 10,000 feet. It is the first of the wonders because its existence makes the other two possible. Hot easterly winds, pregnant with moisture from the Atlantic, move huge cloud masses across the top of the continent, pouring torrents of water on the land below and eventually dropping the rest on the eastern slopes of the mountains. The drenching rains nourish the immense forest that blankets much of Central America and a full third of South America—the largest rain forest in the world. And waters from the ruptured clouds cascade down the slopes of the Andes to feed the most stupendous river system on the face of the earth—the mighty Amazon and its tributaries, seventeen of which are more than a thousand miles long!

But not all of South America is hot and wet. The western slopes of the Andes, brooding out over the Pacific, contain some of the driest areas on earth. And there is cold—Tierra del Fuego, where the continent ends in a curving tip, points to the permanently frozen world of Antarctica, less than 600 miles away. In between the extremes there are fertile highlands and verdant valleys and rolling grasslands, *llanos* in the north and the famed Argentine *pampas* in the south.

The greatest profusion of wildlife in South America occurs in the Amazon River basin and the vast carpet of rain forest, so impenetrable that huge areas have never been seen, certainly not by Westerners and perhaps not even by primitive tribesmen. What treasures of flora and fauna hide there we may discover, as modern technology goes to work carving roads and farmlands out of the exuberant jungle. But if past experience holds true we may regret the discovery, for the opening up of virgin territory may give us knowledge of new life with one hand and snuff out that life with the other.

Preceding pages:
Andean condor
New York Zoological Society

Bald uakari

Endangered Mammals

Giant armadillo | *Priodontes giganteus*
This largest of the armadillos, 40 inches
long without tail and weighing in at 120 pounds,
is remarkably agile and graceful despite its
size; it frequently balances itself on its hind
legs and tail. Its claws are heavy and long, the
one on the middle "finger" measuring a full 7
inches, and it uses them in digging at a furious
rate for ants, termites, snakes, and other
creatures that make up its diet. The giant
armadillo's shell is black except on the head,
tail, and flanks, where the color fades to gray.
The shell is not complete protection—the big
cats and other strong predators can rip off the
plates and bring the animal to an untimely end.
This armadillo formerly ranged over a large
part of the east as well as the Peruvian Amazon,
but now is becoming scarce as these lands
are settled.

Pink fairy armadillo | *Chlamyphorus truncatus*
This smallest and rarest of the armadillos
—only 8 inches long, including tail—is so furtive
and shy that it was virtually unknown, even to
local populations, until discovered by an
American naturalist in 1824. Also called the
lesser pichiciego, it carries 22 pinkish plates
on its upper body for armor, and a broad butt
plate over its rear. The rest of the body is
covered by fine white hairs. It inhabits hot,
sandy areas of western Argentina, leading a
molelike existence in underground tunnels.
When alarmed, it quickly burrows into the earth,
leaving only the butt armor showing, like a cork
in a bottle. It is so rare that recent specimens
for scientific collections were not found by
expeditions, but were gathered during digging
for land reclamation and irrigation projects—a
comment also on why the animal is included
on endangered lists.

Spectacled bear | *Tremarctos ornatus*
The only member of the bear family found
in South America, this small species, only 3½
feet long with a shoulder height of 2½ feet, has
a shaggy black coat with a buff-colored breast
patch and buff across the muzzle and around

Vogt and Specht, *The Mammalia*

Pink fairy armadillo

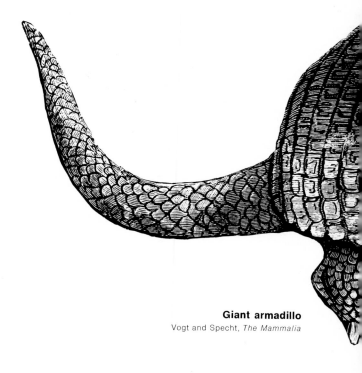

Giant armadillo
Vogt and Specht, *The Mammalia*

the eyes, which explains the name "spectacled." It is also known as the Andean black bear, and is a nimble climber in its mountain forest habitat. A diurnal hunter, it is the least carnivorous of the bears, feeding mostly on leaves, nuts, and fruit. It is now confined to a limited range in Ecuador and northern Peru, and its habitat is shrinking as men move their operations into the Andean forests. There are no estimates of the number of spectacled bears surviving in the wild, but they are known to thrive in captivity and there are now about 50 in zoos.

Marsh deer | *Blastocerus dichotomus*
Largest of the South American deer, the marsh or swamp deer stands 44 inches at the shoulder. It was once common throughout southern Brazil, Paraguay, and northeastern Argentina and may also have ranged into Uruguay. As its name implies, it is never found far from water. Deep red in color, sometimes with patches of black and white, it has 8-point antlers, but 10- and 12-pointers are not rare. In local areas this deer goes under the names *pantanos* and *guazu pucu*.

Pampas deer | *Ozotoceros bezoarticus*
At one time the most abundant deer species on the grasslands of South America, the elegant little pampas deer has fallen victim to disease and encroachment on its habitat, both the result of man's activities. These deer stand about 27 inches at the shoulder, wear a yellowish brown coat, and normally carry 6-pointed antlers. Their decline coincides with the establishment of the cattle industry in South America in the latter half of the nineteenth century. Such diseases as anthrax and hoof-and-mouth found them highly vulnerable, cropping of the tall pampas grass stole their cover, and ranch-fencing prevented them from moving to more hospitable regions. Further development of the grasslands threatens their existence, for they are animals of the open spaces and avoid, as much as possible, mountains and forests.

Jaguar | *Panthera onca*
The largest cat in the Americas, the jaguar prefers the thick cover of dense forests and swamps, but in the northern and southern extremes of its range—the southwestern United

States into Argentina—it can also be found in desert and savanna areas. In those regions of Mexico where it still exists, and in those where it is remembered, it is called *el tigre.* The jaguar is superficially similar to the leopard, but its rosettes tend to be concentrated along the back and have one or more spots in the center. Jaguars are less graceful in appearance than leopards, too, with large heads, heavy bodies, and ponderous stomachs. Like the leopard, however, occasional individuals are melanistic —solid black. They vary in size from 5 to 9 feet, with the tail accounting for about one-third of the length. Good climbers and swimmers, they hunt all sorts of game, including fish and small crocodiles. They rarely attack people, but they are not reluctant to seek an easy meal of domestic stock, and so face the same fate as all the world's big cats.

Amazonian manatee | *Trichechus inunguis*
West Indian manatee | *T. manatus manatus*
Rarely longer than 10 feet, the Amazonian manatee is confined to the fresh waters of the Amazon and Orinoco river basins. It is sometimes called the nailless manatee because the nails on its flippers have

completely atrophied. It has a light spot on its chest, but otherwise is gray black all over. At one time it ranged all along the Atlantic coast of South America, but has been much reduced now by excessive hunting. The West Indian or common manatee ranks as a subspecies with the Florida manatee, but the distinctions between the two are minor. Rarer now, they once ranged from the southeastern United States through much of the Caribbean to northern South America.

Margay | *Felis wiedii*
This attractive spotted feline from the South American forests resembles the ocelot, but is no bigger than a large house cat. In fact, because it tames rather easily, it is gaining popularity as a most unusual household pet— an efficient one, too, for it is an excellent rat killer. It is found mostly in the forests of Brazil and Guiana, where it is locally known as the tiger cat.

Goeldi's marmoset | *Callimico goeldii*
Strictly speaking, this forest dweller of the Upper Amazon River basin, eastern Peru, northern Bolivia, and western Brazil is not a marmoset at all but one of the titi-tamarins. In fact, it is also called Goeldi's tamarin. It looks,

Vogt and Specht, *The Mammalia*

Pampas deer

Amazonian manatee

Margay   Lydekker, *The Royal Natural History*

Goeldi's marmoset

it has been said, as if it were put together from pieces of several other creatures—face and claws of the marmoset, skull and teeth of the spider monkey, and ears of the capuchin monkey. Rare, suspicious, and fast moving, this usually coal black animal with a capelike mane of long hair does not show up often in the world's zoos. It is the sole member of its genus.

Spider monkey | *Ateles geoffroyi frontatus A. g. panamensis*

These two monkeys are subspecies of the Central American spider monkey. One is found primarily in Costa Rica and Nicaragua, and the other in Panama. For the most part reddish, with black areas on the head and the tip of the tail, they belong to a larger group sometimes referred to as "hand-tailed" or "five-handed" monkeys, names earned by their long, prehensile tails, which literally serve as an extra hand. Extremely agile, these monkeys

can perform marvelous acrobatic feats, launching themselves in twenty-foot leaps and landing safely—without looking. Living high in the trees, where they eat leaves and fruits, they rarely descend to earth. They are under pressure as their forest habitat diminishes, and they are also hunted by natives, who trap them alive for sale to zoos, circuses, and medical laboratories and kill them for food. Killing a monkey high in the trees is one thing, but retrieving it is something else again—when it dies its muscles freeze and it will continue to hang there. This is why the Indians tip their arrows with curare; the drug is a muscle-relaxer, and a slain monkey will soon drop to the ground.

Woolly spider monkey | *Brachyteles arachnoides*

The only species of its genus, the woolly spider monkey is also the rarest of American primates

63

Woolly spider monkey
Lydekker, *The Royal Natural History*

Spider monkey
Lydekker, *The Royal Natural History*

and one of the least known. These monkeys of the Tupi Forest and a limited section of coastal mountains in southeastern Brazil may be 22 inches long, with a 27-inch prehensile tail, which is naked in the tactile area near the tip. They weigh about 3½ pounds. On most of them the woolly fur is brown or gray with a yellowish cast, but on some it is reddish. The back of the neck and the forehead are reddish orange, the crown of the head may be chestnut, and the face is often a brilliant red—especially, as in humans, when the animal is excited. These monkeys have been little studied, and science does not know if the color variations are individual, sex-linked, or a product of geographical location. As in true spider monkeys, the limbs are long; thumbs are either vestigial or lacking. Conversion of their forest homeland to agriculture has severely reduced the range of the woolly spider monkeys, and their population is at a precarious level. They do not thrive in zoos, and have never been known to breed in captivity.

Red-backed squirrel monkey | *Saimiri oerstedii*

Also called Oersted's squirrel monkey, this diminutive creature lives in Costa Rica and Panama, where bands of 10 to 100 flit through the trees in search of insects, small birds and eggs, fruits and nuts. They purr like cats when eating and screech when alarmed, but otherwise are quiet, especially for monkeys. Their bodies are about 10 inches long, their tails 14 inches. Their faces are white, but the area around the mouth and nostrils is hairless and black. Although they are basically arboreal, they have been known to drop from the trees to ride, like cowboys in a rodeo, on the backs of wild hogs, apparently for the sheer fun of it.

Ocelot | *Felis pardalis*

The ocelot is one of the most beautiful of the spotted cats, and too many of the animals have given up their lives so that their hides could be made into luxurious fur coats. Their coloring is more varied than on most spotted cats, ranging from golden sand or grayish on the head and down the back to silvery on the sides, with white paws and belly. Black stripes mark

Ocelot

the head and neck, and gray ovals edged in black line the body. The ocelot is sometimes called the painted leopard; "ocelot" itself comes from the Indian *tlalocelotl,* or field tiger. The animal stands about 20 inches at the shoulder and grows to about 4½ feet long, including tail. Although it is a good tree climber, it prefers hunting on the ground for such prey as rodents, small deer, and reptiles, and haunts villages and farms where domestic animals are available for the taking. This habit, together with its beautiful pelt, has made it a ready target for hunters all through its range—at one time from southern Texas and Arizona down through Central America and into Brazil and Bolivia. It is legally protected from hunting now, but is nevertheless in danger of extinction, since laws cannot always be enforced.

Giant otter

Giant otter | *Pteronura brasiliensis*

This largest otter in the world is 7 feet or more in length, including a flat, 3-foot, paddlelike tail that gives it an alternative name, flat-tailed otter. It inhabits the rivers of northern South America, where it burrows in the banks or under tree roots, and feeds largely on fish; in some areas it is called *lobo de rio,* river wolf. Like river otters, it eats its catch on land, but is not really at home in that element; its webbed feet and short legs are much more efficient in the water. The giant otter's fur is usually rich brown fading to light brown on the neck, head, and underparts, and a large creamy white patch marks the chest. Despite the fact that it is diurnal, the otter's habits are not well known, partly because it is so shy a creature—at the first sign of danger it dives into deep water and swims out of the area. The shyness may result from the fact that it has been hunted so relentlessly for its valuable pelt, which at one time carried a price tag of $1,700. Still fairly abundant in some remoter areas of its huge range, the giant otter is not in imminent danger of extinction; but it is already scarce in the greater part of its habitat and it is definitely on the decline.

Gladys Porter Zoo

Jaguar

The Vicuña: Saved

Small members of the camel family living high up in the Andes near the frost line, vicuñas are most famous for their reddish, short-haired coats, which give one of the finest wools in the world. The diameter of each vicuña hair is only 5/10,000 of an inch, half the thickness of the best Australian merino wool—so fine that the fleeces of a dozen animals are needed to make a single yard of cloth.

In the days of the Incas, the vicuña was protected and worshiped as the daughter of Pachmama, the goddess of fertility, and only high officials could hunt it. Garments woven from its wool were worn by royalty and the priestesses of the Temple of the Sun, the wool usually clipped from live animals that were then released. In later years, however, after the fall of the Inca civilization, the sensible religious conservation laws that had been in effect were discarded, and vicuñas were wantonly slaughtered for their meat, hides, and wool.

Surprisingly, there were still 100,000 or so left in 1950, but overhunting became so severe with the demand for vicuña cloth that by the early 1960s, in only a little more than a decade, the population had crashed to 10,000. In 1964, Peru made South American conservation history for the second time by establishing the first vicuña reserve at Pampas Galeras (the first time occurred in 1825 when Simon Bolivar banned the killing of the animal in his country). Other nations in the range of the vicuña began working on their own conservation programs, and Great Britain and the United States led the way in prohibiting the importation of vicuña products. These commonsense measures worked, and the vicuña made a dramatic turnaround, starting on the long comeback trail.

Dr. E. R. Degginger, APSA

Spectacled bear

Spider monkey

Ocelot

Golden lion marmoset

70

Central American tapir

Thin-spined porcupine | *Chaetomys subspinosus*

Another animal feeling the squeeze as Brazil's forests disappear is this already rare porcupine. Although it can climb trees, it lives on the ground in the eastern part of the country. It is dark-colored, with a broad, flat muzzle, and its quills are stiff only in certain areas, such as on its head, neck, shoulders, and the base of the tail. Elsewhere on the body they are more like long, soft bristles. These animals grow to a length of about 30 inches, roughly a third of which is tail.

White-nosed saki | *Chiropotes albinasus*

The saki is a member of a subfamily of monkeys characterized by well-developed brains, nonprehensile tails, and bare faces. There are three species of sakis: the red-backed, the black-bearded, and the white-nosed. It is the latter, a resident of the forests of Brazil, that is most periled.

Brazilian three-toed sloth | *Bradypus torquatus*

Sloths are legendary for the slowness with which they move—they have been clocked at a maximum of thirteen feet a minute along a tree branch and only half that on the ground. They spend most of their lives suspended upside down from branches, clinging with strong, curved claws. They rarely descend to the ground, for here, because of their anatomical structure, they cannot stand or walk, and to move must drag their bodies along. Surprisingly, however, they are able swimmers. Two kinds of brownish hair make up their coat, one short, soft, and woolly, the other longer, stiffer, and grooved. Algae growing on the stiffer guard hairs, particularly during the rainy season, give the sloth a greenish cast and help to camouflage it from predators seeking it high in the trees. Other members of the South American sloth family live in Peru, Ecuador, Bolivia, and Venezuela.

Thin-spined porcupine
Philip Jones

Brazilian three-toed sloth

Mountain tapir

Gladys Porter Zoo

Golden-rumped tamarin | *Leontideus chrysopygus*
Golden-headed tamarin | *L. chrysomelas*
Golden lion marmoset | *L. rosalia*
These three miniature primates of the Brazilian forests have big ears, bright, shiny eyes, and silky hair and are sometimes called maned tamarins. With long, curved claws, instead of monkeylike nails, they climb about in the trees in the manner of squirrels. The golden lion marmoset—or tamarin—is brilliantly colored in deep golden yellow with a metallic sheen. The others show more localized iridescence. These attractive creatures were discovered in 1735 by a French mathematician doing measurements in the equatorial regions.

Brazilian tapir | *Tapirus terrestris*
Central American tapir | *T. bairdii*
Mountain tapir | *T. pinchaque*
Related distantly to horses and rhinos, tapirs look something like large pigs with long snouts; they are so strange looking that people did not believe the descriptions of them brought back by early explorers. In fact, *pinchaque,* the scientific name for the mountain tapir, is an old Indian word that means "mythical monster." There are four species, three in Central and South America and one in Southeast Asia. All tapirs have 4 toes on their front feet and 3 on the hind feet. Plump and chunky, they can weigh up to 800 pounds. Their preferred habitat is wet—rivers and marshy lowlands to mountain forests—where they feed at night on vegetation. The mountain tapir, which, unlike the others, has no mane, is found mostly in the Andes of Colombia and Ecuador; the Brazilian, or American tapir, in Brazil; and the Central American tapir, in parts of Ecuador and Colombia north to Veracruz in Mexico. Tapirs need plenty of water and rain forest to flourish, and widespread deforestation, road construction, and human settlement—together with hunting—have drastically reduced their numbers throughout their range. In 1968 the World Wildlife Fund, basing its estimates on a field research effort, put the number of mountain tapirs at no more than 2,000.

Brazilian tapir

Tiger cat | *Felis tigrina*

The tiger cat is a forest animal of Central and South America, ranging from Honduras to Paraguay, but only east of the Andes. Similar to the ocelot but slightly smaller, its black-banded oval spots are larger, its head is rounder, and its tail is longer. It lives in bands in the trees and preys on birds, small creatures, and domestic animals. Since it resembles the ocelot, it has been hunted for its fur.

Bald uakari | *Cacajao calvus*
Red uakari | *C. rubicundus*
Black uakari | *C. melanocephalus*

Related to the sakis, the uakaris are unique among South American primates in that their tails are short. They live in small groups in tropical forests where the ground is seasonally flooded and are limited to scattered areas in Peru, Colombia, Venezuela, Brazil, and Ecuador. Otherwise agile enough in the trees, they are poor jumpers. Their long, silky hair may be brown, yellow, or red. Their faces are naked, the skin is red or black.

Maned wolf | *Chrysocyon brachyurus*

Considered by some the most beautiful and striking animal in South America, the extremely long-legged maned wolf is called "fox-on-stilts" by the natives. It is a creature of the plains in Brazil, Paraguay, Bolivia, and Argentina, where its long legs help it to move through the tall pampas grass with greater ease and give it a better view of its surroundings. It is not, however, a fast runner, and limits itself to small prey, which it pounces on or digs for—guinea pigs, birds, lizards, and frogs. It also eats fruits and even sugarcane. The maned wolf's soft, long-haired coat is a rich reddish brown, the throat and tip of the tail are white, the mane and "boots" are black. Shy and rare, the animals live alone except at mating time. Their major enemies are people, who hunt them as if they were real wolves, and they were already scarce half a century ago. The advance of civilization has shrunk their habitat, and they have been completely exterminated in some areas. Brazil estimated only about 2,000 left in 1967.

Maned wolf
San Diego Zoo

Gladys Porter Zoo

Red uakari

San Diego Zoo

Black uakari

Red-billed curassow
G. Harrison/Bruce Coleman Inc.

Endangered Birds

Andean condor | *Vultur gryphus*

The largest flying bird in the world, the Andean condor has a wingspread that averages 10 feet and can reach 12 feet. Similar to the California condor but larger, it is mainly glossy black with white upper wing coverts and the typical neck ruff and naked head. The wings of these huge birds are specialized for soaring, and they can do so for hours, spiraling up to heights of 15,000 feet with no apparent effort. They cannot fly, however, unless air currents or thermals are active, which explains their preference for a mountainous habitat, and they are more or less grounded in wet weather. Carrion eaters, they have strong ripping beaks but weak feet. Females lay a single large white egg, usually on the ground, in a stump, or in a cliffside cranny. Incubation takes 6 or 7 weeks, and once hatched, the young are dependent upon their parents for about 8 months. More widespread than their California relatives, Andean condors live at altitudes from 7,000 to 16,000 feet throughout the Andes, from Colombia south to Tierra del Fuego. Less pressured by civilization than the California bird, they have not yet been brought to a crisis situation. But their numbers have dropped considerably from former times, and will undoubtedly decline further with increasing human development of their range.

Red-billed curassow | *Crax blumenbachii*

The local name of this large, dark bird with a crest of curly feathers is *mutu*. Its range is in the deep forests of eastern Brazil, where it lives in the trees and on the ground. Like other curassows, its bill is strong and curved and its wings are short and rounded, suitable for swift but awkward flight through the trees. As long ago as 1954 this bird was believed to be on the road to extinction, and as the Brazilian forests disappear its plight will worsen.

Atitlán grebe | *Podilymbus gigas*

Also called the giant pied-billed grebe, this emphatically aquatic bird lives only in the southwest highlands of Guatemala, its habitat

Atitlán grebe   Philip Jones

the large lake of Atitlán. It has become so adapted to its watery element that its small, weak wings cannot sustain it in flight. A dark, blackish bird, it is twice the size of the common pied-bill grebe. Since 1929, when it was recognized as a separate form, it has maintained a steady population of about 100 pairs on the lake, despite some hunting (illegal since 1959) by local Indians and visiting white gunners. In 1964, however, only 100 birds were counted, and in 1966 the figure dropped to 86. Wildlife specialists fear that the attrition may have been caused by nonnative smallmouth and largemouth bass, introduced into the lake in 1957. Evidence seems to point to the fact that the fish, in addition to competing with the birds for food, make many a meal on defenseless grebe chicks.

Darwin's rhea | *Pterocnemia pennata*

The rheas, large, flightless, running birds related to ostriches, are the giant birds of the Americas. There are two species, and the largest, the common rhea, stands up to 5 feet tall and weighs up to 55 pounds. Darwin's rhea, somewhat smaller, is gray brown spotted with white and ranges the grasslands of Argentina, Peru, Bolivia, and Uruguay. Rheas are often found near rivers and swamps, where they feed on plant material, insects, mollusks, and small vertebrates. Like ostriches, they travel in troops of 20 or 30 and often mingle with herds of deer and cattle. They are excellent swimmers and swift runners—their fluffy feathers, useless for

Darwin's rhea

flight, serve as "tacking sails," enabling them to maneuver quickly, and on the straightaway they can outpace a horse. The ground nest is scraped out and lined by the male, who usually acquires a harem of 6 to 8 females after fighting off other suitors. In displaying for his wives, the male utters distinctly mammallike roars. After the 20 or so eggs are laid, he chases the hens away and incubates the clutch himself. The chicks, hatching in about 40 days, can run almost as soon as they dry out. Rheas have long been hunted by South American Indians and gauchos, but they are being squeezed more now by the demand for space as the lands in which they range are being opened up to development.

Endangered Reptiles

Morelet's crocodile | *Crocodylus moreletii*
Known as the bulbous crocodile, this species is found in Guatemala and the eastern regions of British Honduras. It reaches a length of about 8 feet and becomes almost black in old age. Like the American crocodile, it carries a bulbous dome between the eyes, but its snout is much broader and shorter.

Orinoco crocodile | *Crocodylus intermedius*
This crocodile, the only species limited to South America, is found along the banks of the Orinoco River; hence its name. One of the largest, it reaches a length of 15 feet (some sources say 23 feet) and has a narrower and more elongated snout than other American crocodiles.

South American river turtle | *Podocnemis expansa*
Once so abundant they actually prevented boats from moving freely on the rivers of their range—the Amazon, the Negro, and the Orinoco—the South American river turtles were a staple in the diet of the forest Indians. Old records tell of 20-foot-high piles of eggs collected by foragers. These depredations, coupled with an overkill of the animals for meat and oil, resulted about a century ago in a drastic drop in the population. The turtles retreated to less favorable nesting sites in more isolated regions of Venezuela and Brazil, where they are now legally protected, although enforcement is not adequate in all areas. Artificial nesting sites have been built on Lake Valencia in Venezuela, and there is hope that the turtles will flourish under controlled conditions and once more become a valuable source of protein.

Orinoco crocodile
New York Public Library

Morelet's crocodile

South American river turtle

EUROPE
The Human Habitat

Separated from Asia by a series of
natural boundaries—the Urals,
mountains and river, the Caucasus,
the Caspian and Black seas—Europe
qualifies in geography books as a
continent. But in reality it is a huge peninsula
projecting from the vast mass of Eurasia and is
itself composed of a multitude of peninsulas
within peninsulas. Like black and white
photography, it has two images: From the
landward side it is a series of fingers poking
into the sea, so many that it has the longest
coastline, in proportion to its size, of any of
the continents. But from the seaward side we
see the reverse image—so many fingers of
water projecting into the land that no place on
the entire continent is more than five hundred
miles from the sea.

Europe is capped on the north by the
frigid waters of the Arctic Ocean and the
craggy mountains of Scandinavia. To the south
it is supported by the warm Mediterranean and
a lengthy east-west mountain chain that
includes the Pyrenees, the Alps, the Car-
pathians, and the Balkans. Between the
mountains, from the Atlantic coast of France
to the wall of the Urals, stretches the great
European plain—tundra and forests, lesser
mountains and rocky hills, lakes and freshwater
marshes, steppes and fertile river bottoms.

Compared to other continents, Europe's
store of wildlife is small in both quantity and
dimension. Over the centuries of developing
Western civilization, the land has been
converted almost exclusively into human
habitat, leaving room for relatively few large
animals. But natural events over a much
greater time period had already slowed the
tempo of life there: At least four times in a
million years, invading glaciers came rumbling
down from the Arctic, entombing the land in
dark prisons of ice. Life returned in the gentler
periods when the ice receded, only to be driven
out again and again, denied the unmolested
ages of evolutionary change granted softer
climes. If Europe has fewer endangered
species today than the other land masses, it is
not because her people have been kinder to
their animal brethren; they had fewer to start
with and did away with them earlier.

Bruce Coleman Inc.

Spanish lynx

Endangered Mammals

Pyrenean desman | *Galemys pyrenaicus*
Desmans, similar to large shrews, formerly were widely distributed over Europe but now are reduced to two relict populations, one in the area of the Caspian Sea and the other in the Pyrenees and northern Portugal. Members of the mole family that have adapted to an aquatic existence, they have webbed toes, long, waterproof guard hairs to protect the dense underfur, a scaly tail, and a long snout, which they use much as an elephant uses its trunk. The snout, a striking feature, is waved about to investigate food and may even be used as a snorkel when the animal is submerged. These little creatures live in burrows along rivers and streams and eat insects, larvae, fish, crustaceans, and worms. The threatened Pyrenean desman, 4 to 5 inches long, is restricted to a shrinking range in the Pyrenees in both France and Spain, and in the mountains of northern Portugal. An ancient creature, which has survived the ages unchanged by virtue of the fact that it fills a specialized ecological niche largely unchallenged by either predators or competitors, it is in trouble now because of changes to its habitat. Unlike its Caspian relative, it prefers cold, clean, fast-moving water, conditions being altered more and more by pollution and dam construction.

Pyrenean ibex | *Capra pyrenaica pyrenaica*
This animal, one of seven species of a type of wild goat living in high mountains, stands about 30 inches high, weighs about 100 pounds, and has long, back-curved horns marked by evenly spaced knots. It is distinctive among the ibex for its coloring, which is more like a true goat's, with black flanks, legs, and face, and a white belly. During the Middle Ages and before, ibex were plentiful throughout the Pyrenees and were hunted for their meat, which was considered a delicacy. In time, especially after the introduction of rifles and shotguns, the animals became scarcer, until by the beginning of this century there were no more than a dozen left. Legal protection was finally granted to the ibex in 1959, and the population has risen slightly to 24 or so, all limited to the Mount Perdida area in Spain's Huasca Province.

Pyrenean desman
Philip Jones

Pyrenean ibex

Spanish lynx | *Felis lynx pardina*

Lynxes and wildcats were once the most numerous felines to be found in Europe's forests, the European lynx to the north and the Spanish lynx over the greater part of the Iberian Peninsula and into the Pyrenees. Bob-tailed members of the cat family, lynxes are about 3 feet long, covered with thick brown fur spotted with black, and wear characteristic "side-burns." The European lynx has been exterminated over much of its range, and the Spanish race is even rarer, surviving only in Spain's Coto Doñana Reserve, in the delta of the Guadalquivir, and possibly in parts of the Pyrenees and Portugal. Numbers are estimated at perhaps 200. Factors governing the decline of the lynx include extensive deforestation throughout much of its range, and the fact that it has been—and still is, outside the Coto Doñana reserve—classified as vermin, subject to "killing on sight."

Cyprian mouflon | *Ovis orientalis ophion*

This wild sheep native to the island of Cyprus in the Mediterranean stands 26 inches at the shoulder and wears a reddish brown coat and a black throat mane; males carry heavy, 3-sided horns shaped like sickles and measuring as much as 2 feet around the curve. Plentiful during the Middle Ages, mouflon were chased by hunters running both hounds and trained cheetahs. The hunting continued in less spectacular fashion in succeeding centuries, and by the end of the 1800s the numbers of mouflon were sorely depleted. The survivors retreated into deep forests and the southern mountains, but increasing human population and development of the island added to the animal's woes, especially since there was no real effort to curtail hunting. In 1936, some 25 to 30 mouflon were counted in the Troodos Forest; the next year they were gone, and the total population consisted of 15 animals in the Paphos Forest. Then conservation organizations, alerted to the plight of the creature, succeeded in having the entire Paphos Forest declared a reserve, with firearms banned for any purpose. Protection was given to the mouflon, wardens were appointed, the large flocks of domestic goats that had roamed the forest, accompanied by herdsmen who had raged relentless war on the wild sheep, were excluded from the woodland, and the mouflon began a comeback. Unfortunately, however, political problems on Cyprus in recent years, leading to armed conflict and unenforced laws, have resulted in further decimation of the mouflon population. Accurate counts are unavailable, but it is believed that the animals number no more than 200 today, if that many.

Spanish lynx
Philip Jones

Cyprian mouflon

Endangered Birds

Spanish imperial eagle | *Aquila heliaca adalberti*

A magnificent hunting bird, once distributed widely over western Europe and into North Africa at least to the Atlas Mountains, the imperial eagle is now restricted to a relatively small area of mountains in central and southern Spain. It was seen occasionally in Morocco and Algeria until the 1960s, but may be extinct there now. At last count, only about 100 birds survived, with only 7 active nests in the Coto Doñana Reserve. The fate of the birds outside the reserve, where they are subject to hunting, nest raiding, and the pressures of civilization, is precarious. Even when undisturbed in the wild, a breeding pair will raise only one chick a year, and very few hawks or eagles have ever bred in captivity.

Audouin's gull | *Larus audouinii*

Most gulls are notorious scavengers, noisily squabbling over any tidbit of food they can find on the beach, near ships, in harbors and town dumps. Audouin's gull differs from the norm, however, in that it prefers deep waters and feeds on small fish it catches at sea. This habit may be one of the factors contributing to the bird's decline, for it nests on several small Mediterranean islands side by side with the

Vogt and Specht, *The Mammalia*

Spanish imperial eagle

Audouin's gull

Philip Jones

similar Mediterranean herring gull, which is abundant—and in no way fastidious about its eating habits. Audouin's gull, which can be distinguished from similar gulls by its prominent red bill with a black bar, its white head and black wingtips, is confined to the Mediterranean, where it formerly had a wide distribution. In the last half century its population has steadily dropped and is estimated now at fewer than 1,000 birds. They are rarely seen near sandy coasts, and most records are from rocky islets where they still breed—off Morocco, Tunisia, Corsica, and Cyprus and in the Aegean. Egg stealing by fishermen and collectors—and perhaps by the not so neighborly herring gull—probably is contributing to the bird's decline. Its condition is so precarious that, if it is to be saved, the nations controlling its nesting sites must give it as much protection as possible.

The Great Auk: Lost

For thousands of years the great auk, a penguinlike bird of the North Atlantic, was hunted and eaten by man. The auk flourished despite this early cropping, however, and despite the fact that the female laid only one enormous 5-inch egg a season. Reports from past centuries suggest that there must have been literally millions of birds on the rocky nesting islets and coastal cliffs from Newfoundland across to Scandinavia. In 1534 a French ship captain, Jacques Cartier, landed on Funk Island off Newfoundland, the largest breeding ground. In a half hour, he boasted, his men killed enough of the birds to fill two longboats, and slaughtered at least a thousand more during the long day.

There were many more long days to come for the great auk, a large bird up to 3 feet tall. Graceful only in the water, where its stubby wings served as stabilizers as it dived in search of fish, it was unable to fly, slow and clumsy on land, and totally defenseless. Using only sticks and paddles as bludgeons, ship's crews hungering for meat slew thousands, and local fishermen regularly raided the colonies, eating their fill of flesh and boiling down the rest of their catch into cooking oil.

By the early years of the nineteenth century the huge colony on Funk Island was wiped out, and attention was turned to a second large nesting ground on Geirfuglasker, also known as Penguin Island, near Iceland. Here the pattern of carnage was repeated, as ships sailed from Reykjavik for the express purpose of harvesting the birds as food. That commerce came to an abrupt end in 1830, for something stirred in the bowels of the earth and Geirfuglasker slipped beneath the icy waters. The few remaining great auks sought haven on Eldey, a nearby speck of rock, but the attacks went on, for the collectors were interested now that the bird had all but disappeared, and large sums were offered for great auk skins.

The end came in 1844. Responding to a cash offer by a Reykjavik agent, a fisherman named Vilhjalmur Hakonarsson gathered a small crew and set sail for Eldey. There he found only two great auks, a mated pair—the last on the face of the earth. He killed them both, and in the excitement of the ''hunt,'' someone stepped on the single egg in the nest.

Lydekker, *The Royal Natural History*

AFRICA
Animal Paradise
and Cradle of Life

Dian Fossey/Bruce Coleman Inc.

Africa has always held a special fascination for Westerners, primarily because of the almost unbelievable diversity and richness of its animal life. We flock to see the creatures in zoos; but no isolated specimen in sterile surroundings can evoke the same feeling as seeing the animal in its natural setting—for Africa itself is a land of spectacular habitats.

Geologically ancient and stable, the continent has remained more or less unchanged for the past 600 million years. It is essentially a great plateau, creased by the Great Rift valley in the east and studded with soaring peaks: Kilimanjaro's famous snow-capped cone, the Atlas Range along the Mediterranean, and the Ruwenzori between Lakes Albert and Edward, called the "Mountains of the Moon" by the ancients, who considered them the source of the Nile, and famous for their gigantic vegetation and ice—high glaciers on the Equator.

From the Great Rift valley and the East African highlands west to the Atlantic coast, the heartland is blanketed in thick tropical rain forest centered around the Congo basin, a vast green area of approximately 1½ million square miles. Once the forest was even larger, but it has been replaced now, north and south, by wide, grassy plains. This is the Africa of the tourist, for it is here that the taut drama of life and death is played by a cast of thousands: zebras, giraffes, and antelope of every description; lions, leopards, cheetahs, and packs of wild dogs; hyenas, jackals, vultures, and other scavengers; with supporting players ranging from ponderous elephants and rhinos down to the smallest predators.

On its perimeter, the savanna gives way to scrub forest, wooded steppes, and swamplands. Then come the deserts, desolate Kalahari and Namib in the south, and in the north the overwhelming Sahara, which reaches from the Atlantic 1,250 miles to the Red Sea and into the Middle East—the largest and hottest desert on the face of the earth. Even here, in Africa's harshest environment, various forms of life have found their niches—scorpions and reptiles, yes, but also mammals such as the addax, which never drinks water, making do on whatever moisture it can obtain from the scant desert vegetation it eats.

Mountain gorilla

Preceding pages:
Walia ibex
Holy Land Conservation Fund, Inc.

Endangered Mammals

Addax | *Addax nasomaculatus*
A true desert dweller, the addax survives under conditions that would be impossible for most other animals, obtaining its only moisture from the scant plants making up its diet. In summer its coat is sandy above and white below; in winter it turns gray. A brown patch marks the forehead; the horns twist spirally up to a height of 40 inches, which is also the height of the animal at the shoulders. Adjusted well to its habitat, this antelope has developed big, splayed hooves for easier movement on sand. The addax once ranged the entire desert region between the Nile and the Atlantic Ocean, from the Mediterranean coast south to Nigeria and Cameroon. Overhunting, especially since the introduction of modern repeating firearms, has brought it to the doorway of extinction. It has been exterminated in Egypt, Tunisia, Rio de Oro, and most other areas of its range,

including Tripolitania, where Italian troops, occupying the land a few decades ago, as they rode by in their military caravans machine-gunned herd after herd. Today there are about 5,000 addax left in a vast, waterless area of the western Sahara, near Mauritania and Mali, where they are still hunted by three tribes of nomads. Proposals have been made for a refuge to preserve both the addax and the scimitar-horned oryx, but so far nothing has been done. Fortunately, the addax breeds well in captivity, and it may survive there even if nowhere else.

It is questionable whether or not the addax actually ranged into Palestine in ancient times, but since it is mentioned in the Bible it is one of the animals being bred at Israel's Hai Bar Wildlife Reserve, in the Negev Desert some twenty-five miles north of the Red Sea port of Eilat. Other rare creatures being preserved in this ambitious conservation project include onagers, Nubian ibex, ostriches, Arabian and scimitar-horned oryxes, and Syrian water buffalo, all biblical animals.

Addax

Giant sable antelope | *Hippotragus niger variani*

Magnificent scimitar-curving horns—the record length is 64⅞ inches—have proved to be the undoing of the giant sable antelope, probably the most beautiful of Africa's antelope family. Restricted to central Angola in the vicinity of the Cuanza and Luando rivers, the animal was not discovered until 1913, the last of the large African mammals to be identified by science. In maturity, bulls are glossy black with white underparts, white face markings, and jet black manes; cows, with smaller horns, are a brilliant golden chestnut. Considering their restricted range, these antelopes probably never were numerous. But even with the limited protection granted them in 1926 by the Angolan government, their horns made such splendid trophies—and fetched such exceptionally high prices—that their numbers soon dwindled. Today there are probably no more than 500 to 700 left, most of them living in the Luando and Cangandala reserves, where hunting is strictly prohibited.

Nubian wild ass | *Equus asinus africanus*
Somali wild ass | *E. a. somalicus*

The Nubian wild ass stands about 4 feet at the shoulder and is marked by a narrow stripe running along its spine, a shorter stripe at right angles across the withers, and dark patches on the front fetlocks. In color it is usually gray to fawn. The Somali race is somewhat larger, has similar coloring, but lacks the withers stripe and adds dark, horizontal stripes on its legs. Three subspecies of wild asses once roamed the deserts and arid areas of northern Africa. One, the Algerian wild ass, was extinct in Roman times, about A.D. 300. The other two races are facing the same fate, their decline brought about not only by hunting but by interbreeding with domestic donkeys gone wild, and by competition from domestic stock for the scant vegetation available in the arid area of their range. Estimates put 200 or 300 Nubian asses in the Danakil region of Ethiopia, and a few pockets in other areas, but there is some question as to whether these latter are pure-bred animals. The Somali wild ass may be slightly better off, with

Giant sable antelope

a herd of about 300 in Ethiopia and small groups scattered elsewhere, and perhaps considerably better off, if unconfirmed reports of several herds in Eritrea are true.

Beira | *Dorcatragus megalotis*

Very little is known about this small antelope, which stands less than 2 feet high and weighs in at only about 20 pounds. Its coarse hair is reddish gray in the back, giving way to white on the belly, fawn on the legs, and yellow red on the head. A dark brown stripe marks the flanks. The horns, up to 5 inches long, are worn only by the male. The animal's coloration blends efficiently into the background of its arid environment, almost always a rocky hill, where from 4 to 7 individuals will establish their territory. Gristly pads on the undersides of the hooves enable them to move easily over the stony surface; dew and vegetation apparently supply them with water. They are said to be the only dwarf antelopes to live in groups. They range primarily in mountainous regions of Somalia, and perhaps in parts of Ethiopia.

Bontebok

Pygmy chimpanzee

Bontebok | *Damaliscus dorcas dorcas*

The bontebok and its relative the blesbok rank with the fastest antelopes in Africa. Both run low to the ground, fully extended. The bontebok is basically reddish brown with white legs below the knee and a brown stripe on the forelegs. The face is white, as is the rump patch, and the lyre-shaped horns are 16 inches long. In the seventeenth century, when Europeans arrived in South Africa, the bontebok was abundant in a strip of land in the southwest corner of Cape Province. As the Boer settlements flourished, the antelope declined, a victim of hunting and theft of its habitat. It probably would have gone extinct had not a large landowner, Alexander Van der Byl, driven a herd of about 300 into an enclosed area on his farm in the year 1864. His neighbor, Dr. Albertyn, did the same, followed by other farmers. This action saved the animal, but poaching and disease took their toll and the herds dwindled. In 1931, the 1,784-acre National Bontebok Park was established and

Beira
Philip Jones

Somali wild ass

104

stocked with 22 animals, but constant flooding on the land brought parasitic infections and retarded the recovery of the bontebok. In 1961, therefore, the surviving animals were transferred to a better situated park, and additional land was set aside as a reserve. Numbers grew, and today there are about 750 bontebok in Cape Province, the largest concentration on a private farm and the next largest in the national park.

Pygmy chimpanzee | *Pan paniscus*
According to some sources, the pygmy chimpanzee was first discovered in 1929 in a small section of humid rain forest south of the Congo River in Central Africa, and the first specimens to reach a Western zoo arrived in 1936. Other sources say the British Museum had a specimen as early as 1895, that New York's Bronx Zoo exhibited one in 1923, and that an animal described way back in 1758 was undoubtedly a pygmy chimpanzee. This difference of opinion extends to classification of the creature, some holding that it is merely a variation of the familiar chimp, *Pan troglodytes,* and others maintaining that it differs enough to be placed in a separate genus. Despite the confusion, this much is sure: not a great deal is known about the pygmy chimpanzee. Physically, it differs considerably from other chimps. It is less than half as big, about 2 feet tall; its legs and torso are longer, proportionately, its shoulders and feet narrower; its entire coat is black except for a white rump patch, its lips are red instead of gray or black, and its second and third toes have grown together. There are no estimates of numbers in the wild, but the animal's habitat is limited, making it highly vulnerable to forest destruction. Another danger facing the pygmy chimp, as well as other chimps, is the possibility of increased demand for organs to be transplanted into human beings—chimpanzee kidneys, for example, survive in transplant for as long as two months while those of other monkeys last only ten days.

Tana River red colobus | *Colobus badius rufomitratus*
Zanzibar red colobus | *C. b. kirkii*
The colobus, or guereza, is the only

Zanzibar red colobus
Philip Jones

leaf-eating monkey in Africa and is distinguished from the related Asiatic langur by its lack of a thumb. These animals range between 20 and 27 inches in height, with a tail of similar length, and come in versions of black and white, all black, olive, and red. The Tana River red colobus is rust-colored on the top of its head, but much of the rest of the body is gray, grayish yellow, and shades of olive and brown. It has been much hunted for its spectacular pelt, but the major reason for its declining numbers is widespread destruction of the forest along the lower Tana River in Kenya, where it lives in the tops of trees. The Zanzibar red colobus, with reddish brown head, back, and shoulders, black hands and feet, and yellowish white forehead and cheeks, is just as tree-oriented as the other members of his family, the most arboreal of all African monkeys, and is in danger largely because of habitat loss to human activities on its restricted island home.

Jentink's duiker | *Cephalophus jentinki*
The name duiker is Afrikaans and means ''diver,'' an apt description of these small, shy

105

Jentink's duiker

forest antelopes that literally dive into the undergrowth at the slightest sound. They are found in brush country and forest throughout much of Africa below the Sahara, but are seldom seen. Rarest of them all is Jentink's duiker, one of the largest of the several races, which is marked by a wide white collar on its forequarters separating the gray body from a black head. Only a few of these duikers have ever been seen by Western man, and for a long time they were believed to range only in Liberia. Other information suggests that they can also be found in the Ivory Coast and Sierra Leone, where native hunters seek them for their meat and tough hides. The only known specimen in captivity at this writing is a young female named Alpha in the zoo in Brownsville, Texas. Little is known of the animal's habits in the wild, but zoo officials say duikers are high-strung and delicate, fully capable, if startled, of crashing head-on into a wall. Duikers are one of the few ruminants to eat meat— Alpha's diet consists of a mixture of grains, grass, vegetables, and dog food.

Western giant eland | *Taurotragus derbianus derbianus*
Also called Lord Derby's eland, this is a beautiful animal, with a dark red coat marked by 14 or 15 vertical white stripes on the side, a broad black dorsal stripe, a long brown mane tipped with white, and massive twisted horns that may be almost 4 feet long. With a shoulder height of about 70 inches, it is the largest of antelopes and has long been hunted for its tender meat, its fat content, and its valuable hide. Attempts have been made to domesticate the giant eland, but its ability to leap fences as high as six feet, or break through all but the stoutest barriers when the migration urge arises, proved to be drawbacks. The animal's susceptibility to the scourge of domesticated cattle, rinderpest, also discouraged these early attempts and is undoubtedly a contributing factor in the scarcity of giant elands today. Once rather widely distributed in West Africa, the giant eland has been reduced to no more than a few dozen animals in isolated pockets from Senegal to southwest Sudan.

Pygmy hippopotamus

Clarke's gazelle | *Ammodorcas clarkei*

This now rare gazelle, also called dibatag, is confined to the arid interior of Somalia and Ethiopia. Its height at the shoulder is 35 inches, and its horns curve evenly up and forward, attaining a length of 12 inches in large, mature specimens. It is generally colored a dark, purplish red, with white streaks on the face and a fawn-colored neck, white belly, and long, slender black tail. Travelers in the area of its range in the latter part of the nineteenth century reported numerous herds, but by 1935 the animal was reduced to "localized and rare" status, most likely because of overhunting.

Vogt and Specht, *The Mammalia*

Clarke's gazelle
Philip Jones

Dorcas gazelle

Cuviers gazelle | *Gazella cuviera*

As long ago as the 1930s this was considered probably the rarest of all the gazelles. This fawn-colored animal, with a broad black stripe on each side of the rump and strongly ribbed horns curving back, then forward at the tip, was formerly found in abundance in Morocco, Algeria, and Tunisia, in the Atlas Mountains, on the border of the Sahara, and in the highlands eastward. It was slaughtered mercilessly, however, by native tribesmen, by shepherds in the high pastures, and by automobile-borne hunting parties. Today it barely survives in remote sections of Morocco and Tunisia.

Dorcas gazelle | *Gazella dorcas*

An indistinct dark stripe along the flanks separates the reddish brown upper parts of this gazelle from the sandy white color below. One of the smallest of the gazelles, it stands only 22 inches at the shoulders; its horns are about 13 inches long. It lives in the inhospitable desert and arid plains regions of North Africa and Saudi Arabia, where it manages to get by without water for long periods of time as long as there is adequate vegetation to eat.

Mhorr gazelle | *Gazella dama mhorr*

Mhorr gazelles, ranging in southern Morocco into the stony deserts of the Sahara,

Slender-horned gazelle | *Gazella leptoceros leptoceros*
G. l. marica

Both races of this medium-size gazelle are endangered, *marica* on the Arabian peninsula and *leptoceros* in its widespread range in the Sudan, Egypt, Libya, and Algeria. Also known as the rhim or Loder's gazelle, this animal stands about 40 inches tall, weighs about 60 pounds, has long, thin, almost straight horns, and a much lighter fawn coloring than other gazelles. Since so much of its habitat consists of desert wastes, its hooves are splayed for easier movement on the sand. In neither northern Africa nor Arabia are the animals protected, and hunting parties—often motorized in recent decades—have succeeded in placing them in serious jeopardy. If the slender-horned gazelle survives, it will probably be because it can exist in a harsh environment penetrated by few forms of life that might harm it.

Mountain gorilla | *Gorilla gorilla beringei*

The biggest of the apes, the gorilla averages almost 6 feet tall when standing upright and tips the scales at about 400 pounds. In the easy life of captivity, however, males often balloon up to 600 or 700 pounds. Gorillas have short legs, barrel-shaped chests, and mighty arms with a span of about 8 feet. Their feet are similar to those of humans, for they spend much of their time on the ground where they can find the juicy plant stems that are their preferred food. Their fingers are short and stubby, and they usually move about on all fours in what is called "knuckle-walking." This is somewhat inaccurate as a description, however, for the weight rests on the middle phalanges of the fingers rather than on the knuckles. The gorilla's skin is jet black, the hair is black to brown gray, and adult males grow a silvery saddle on the back. Like people, gorillas grow gray with age. There are two races, the mountain gorilla and the lowland gorilla, and the most obvious mark that distinguishes them is the crest of hair on the former. The lowland gorilla is restricted to the Congo River basin and is not in danger at the moment. The mountain gorilla, however, living

were zealously sought by native hunters for the bezoars they produced—concretions found in the stomachs and intestines of certain ruminants and considered, in Oriental medicine, to be antidotes to poison. In Morocco, these substances were known as the *Baid-al-Mhorr*—the "eggs of the Mhorr." These gazelles, measuring about 30 inches at the shoulder, are yellow gray or yellow brown animals with the color of the upper parts extending as a tapering stripe down the white legs to the hoofs; their black horns curve back, out, and abruptly forward at the tips. If they still exist, these striking animals will be found only in the harshest inland regions.

in a number of isolated areas over a wide range on the slopes of the Virunga Volcanoes and other montane forest regions of the eastern Congo and parts of Uganda and Rwanda, is under mounting pressure. Expanding human settlement is cutting into the great ape's habitat, and many thousands of acres of forest have disappeared. In recent years, 75 percent of the mountain gorillas in the region of the Virunga Volcanoes were reported slain by poachers. In some areas, tribesmen kill the animals for food, and trappers of animals for zoos and medical institutions sometimes follow the odious practice of slaying the females to capture the defenseless young alive. Several reserves have been set aside for the animals, but political pressure from agriculturists has taken some of the best habitat away—at a time when more should be added if the largest of the primates is to be saved.

Hunter's hartebeest | *Damaliscus hunteri*

A generally uniform rufous coat covers this hartebeest, highlighted by white around the eyes and on the belly and tail; the black, heavily ringed horns curve out and back. About 4 feet tall at the shoulder, Hunter's hartebeest is found in a narrow strip of semi-arid country near the north bank of the Tana River in Kenya and extending into Somalia. The total population, estimated at about 1300 in Kenya and 200 in Somalia, probably has not declined appreciably in recent decades, since local tribes do not consider their hides valuable enough to warrant hunting. They are on the endangered list, however, because of a proposal to settle 75,000 African families in the area and tap the river for irrigation purposes, a move that would certainly put the animal under severe threat. In an effort to dilute the effects of the project, should it be implemented, a small herd of hartebeests was established by airlift in Tsavo National Park. The transfer, dubbed ''Operation Antelope,'' seemed to have failed when two years went by and the animals were not seen again. But in 1966 a tiny herd was spied, 4 of them juveniles.

Swayne's hartebeest | *Alcelaphus buselaphus swaynei*

One of the smallest of the still living hartebeests, Swayne's has a deep reddish brown body, with dark markings on its face and the upper parts of its legs. Its horns vary in shape and size. When these animals were discovered in 1892 there were immense herds darkening the plains of Somalia and parts of Ethiopia, but by 1905 only an estimated 880 still lived, last survivors of the rinderpest epidemics that swept the countryside. Following on the heels of this calamity came civil strife in Somalia and an invasion by opportunistic hunters from Ethiopia, and by the time the smell of gunpowder had blown away, almost all the hartebeest and oryx herds were gone. Today, Swayne's hartebeest is extinct in the Somali Republic, while Ethiopia can count only 200 in a herd on the Alledeghi Plains, plus a few scattered groups haunting the shores of several lakes.

Swayne's hartebeest
Lydekker, *The Royal Natural History*

Pygmy hippopotamus | *Choeropsis liberiensis*

The pygmy hippopotamus looks like the juvenile of the common hippo, or, if you are domestically minded, like a large pig—to which, of course, hippos are distantly related. Adults are about 6 feet long and 2½ feet tall and weigh up to 500 pounds. The animal has a

Preceding pages:
White rhinoceros
Dr. E. R. Degginger, APSA

small head and relatively long legs; its color is a shiny blue black. The pygmy hippo is found only in the swampy forests of West Africa, primarily in Liberia, Sierra Leone, Guinea, and the Ivory Coast. It is nocturnal, and although it swims well it spends less time in the water than its much larger cousin. It is also less inclined to form herds, traveling mostly alone or in pairs, a fact that may explain why naturalists often spend days in the wild without spying one of the creatures. In fact, little is known of the pygmy's life in the wild, except that it is rare and is disappearing at an alarming rate—apparently the victim, in some areas at least, of native hunters who relish its porklike flesh. Fortunately, the animal breeds and thrives well in captivity, and a large zoo-bank has been developed for which a studbook is being prepared.

Gladys Porter Zoo

Pygmy hippopotamus

Barbary hyena | *Hyaena hyaena barbara*
Brown hyena | *H. brunnea*
Nobody's favorite animals, hyenas labor under a reputation that is as unjustified as it is unsavory. Like alligators and vultures, they are the sanitary engineers of the world of nature, cleaning up after some other animal has made

a kill and helping immensely to keep their habitat tidy. But their appearance works against them—ugly, shaggy-haired creatures that look hunchbacked with their forequarters higher than the hind—and their howls and demented chuckles give humans the chills. As a result, they are killed indiscriminately, as if they were truly vermin. The striped hyena, smallest of the races, with a 4-foot body and an 18-inch tail, has a gray or brownish coat broken by almost black stripes, and a crest of longer, erectile hairs down the spine. It ranges from North Africa through Asia Minor to India and is fairly plentiful. But a subspecies, the Barbary race, now limited to Morocco, is in trouble. The brown hyena, a little larger, has a grayish head, a dark coat with indistinct stripes, and dark rings around its lower legs. It ranges in southern Africa, living near the shore and dining on anything left behind by the receding tide, from crabs amd mollusks to the moldering carcass of a beached whale. In some areas, this beachcomber is also known as the strand wolf, and despite its notable efforts in keeping the shoreline clean it is most unwelcome where humans gather.

Walia ibex | *Capra walie*
This wild goat, also called the Abyssinian ibex, lives in a craggy habitat high up in the spectacularly beautiful Semien Mountains of Ethiopia. About 38 inches tall, it carries massive scimitar horns that can measure 45 inches along the curve. It is reddish brown in color, with black stripes on its grayish legs. Local tribes have always hunted the ibex for its hide and meat as well as its horns, which make excellent drinking cups, but the animal received considerable natural protection from its rugged and isolated habitat. The Italian occupation of the country several decades ago brought modern repeating rifles into play, however, and many guerilla fighters, well armed, hid in the mountains and lived off the land—and off the ibex. The end of World War II brought peace and the departure of the occupying forces, but no peace for the ibex, for local hunters were now better armed than ever before and the protective laws imposed by the Ethiopian government were and are largely ignored. An

Brown hyena

additional hazard includes devastation of the habitat as settlers move up the mountainsides to plow the sloping land and run their herds of livestock, practices that lead to widespread erosion. There are now only a few hundred walia ibex left, and their ability to survive is questionable unless the government moves quickly to establish a reserve and provide the animals with enforced protection.

Black lechwe | *Kobus leche smithemani*
A relative of the waterbuck, the black lechwe is a type of antelope that formerly numbered in the hundreds of thousands in Zambia, ranging through the swampy lands around Lake Bangweulu. The development of copper mines in the area, however, brought human settlement and an ever-increasing demand for meat. The hunters were happy to oblige, and since the turn of the century a wide variety of game animals has been all but exterminated in the area. The black lechwe, down to about 4,000 individuals in 1966, has been particularly hard hit, for it exists in no other region. Killing of the last one will spell *finis* for the subspecies.

Barbary leopard

Barbary leopard | *Panthera pardus panthera*
Leopards are the most widely distributed
of the big cats and can be found throughout
Africa, the Middle East, the Caucasus, and
India and up into China, Korea, Manchuria, and
Siberia. They are also probably the smartest
and most adaptable of the cats, making
themselves at home in all kinds of habitat, from
tropical rain forests to dry, open savanna to
high mountain slopes. They are smaller than
lions and tigers, averaging about 7 feet in
length, including tail, and weighing about 100
pounds, although specimens up to 200 pounds
have been recorded. The coat is usually dark
yellow marked by black rosettes; melanistic
forms, all black, are called panthers and once
were believed to constitute a separate species.
Interestingly, the melanistic forms seem to be
found most often in areas where rainfall is
heavy. Wily hunters, leopards prey on deer,
monkeys, antelope, baboons, large rodents,
birds, and other types of small to medium-size
game, and seem to have a special fondness
for domesticated dogs, even entering human
settlements to carry off a meal. Occasionally
they turn into man-eaters, usually when they

Black lechwe

Philip Jones

116

cannot capture other game; the record for a man-eating cat is held by an Indian leopard that killed 125 people before being shot. Leopards are far more troublesome, however, as killers of livestock, and farmers wage incessant war against them.

The Barbary leopard, one of the large races, ranges through Morocco, Algeria, and Tunisia and was still fairly plentiful only a few decades ago. Today, however, its numbers have been greatly reduced, and it is estimated that only about 100 survive in the forests of the Central Atlas in Morocco. There are no estimates available for the other countries, but leopards are known to live still in Akfadou National Park in Algeria, and very likely in some remote mountain regions of Tunisia. Several factors have brought the agile tree-climber to this sorry state. As its natural prey has dwindled, usually because of human activities, it has had to turn more and more to feeding off domestic herds, an activity not treated lightly by well-armed shepherds and stockmen. Even worse for the leopard, its beautiful pelt is highly prized—and priced—and illegal hunting may wipe the animal out despite protective laws.

Tana River mangabey | *Cercocebus galeritus galeritus*

There are 4 species of mangabeys, subdivided into about 10 races, inhabiting the forests south of the Sahara in Africa. Closely related to baboons, they are large, robust monkeys, up to 2 feet long, with long tails that they carry high over the back. The tail is not prehensile, but the mangabeys often curl it around a limb to steady themselves. Of them all, the rarest and most endangered is the Tana River race, an agile animal with long, gray green hair, dark brown at the tips, yellowish on the sides of the head and inner sides of the limbs, with yellowish rings on the tail and a fringe of longer hair on the forehead. This list of physical characteristics is based on the original description of the monkey, made in 1879, because very little has been recorded since that time. The first specimen was obtained at the confluence of the Tana and Osi rivers in Kenya, and only a few people have seen living animals —apparently always on the south side of the

river's reaches. Unfortunately, the narrow strip of gallery forest extending along the riverbanks, rarely more than a few hundred yards wide, is surrounded by country almost desertlike. Expanding into the fertile strip in recent years, local tribes have hacked and burned the forest for many miles along both banks to open spaces for cultivation, and the habitat of the mangabeys and other creatures of the forest has been severely diminished, rendering their position precarious.

Mountain nyala
Philip Jones

Mountain nyala | *Tragelaphus buxtoni*

Largest of the bushbucks, the mountain nyala is a handsome short-haired antelope standing 4½ feet at the shoulder and weighing about 450 pounds. The male boasts gently curving and twisting horns up to 44 inches long. The coat is grayish brown with white markings on the chin, throat, and chest, white vertical stripes on the back, a few white spots on the flanks, and a dorsal crest black above the shoulders and white farther down the back. Discovered as recently as 1908 in the mountains of southern Ethiopia, the mountain nyala was eagerly sought by naturalists and sportsmen, the former to learn more about this interesting new specimen and the latter to take a magnificent new trophy. To find the animal they had to traverse some extremely difficult country, for the mountain nyala lives at altitudes

117

Scimitar-horned oryx

118

above 9,000 feet, in the high forest and up to higher heathland, where the sun burns down during the day and the temperature falls almost to the freezing point at night. It was once thought that only a few thousand mountain nyala were left, but a joint survey by the World Wildlife Fund and the American National Geographic Society in 1966 estimated the number at at least 4,500 and possibly 10,000. Despite this seemingly great population, the animal is not well protected and is much victimized by illegal hunters.

Scimitar-horned oryx | *Oryx tao*

During the Middle Ages the scimitar-horned oryx was so plentiful in its range—around the fringes of deserts and in the arid regions of northern Africa from the Nile to Senegal—that a local king in the Rio de Oro area was said to have presented a visiting dignitary with 1,000 shields covered with the animal's hide. Even a century ago it was still abundant in parts of Morocco, Algeria, and Tunisia, but today it has disappeared from almost all its range, except for a narrow strip along the bottom of the

Lydekker, *The Royal Natural History*

White rhinoceros

Sahara from Mauretania to the Red Sea. This 450-pound animal, with curved horns that are often more than 40 inches long, stands about 4 feet tall and is basically white, with a touch of chestnut on the face, belly, neck, shoulders, and the upper parts of the legs. Its meat is said to compare favorably to top-quality beef, and as a result the animal has been much hunted, especially by a tribe in northern Chad, known as the Haddad, whose life and culture depend exclusively on the oryx. Other nomadic tribes also hunt the beast, and in more recent years carnage has resulted from expeditions of motorized troops and oil prospectors, all well armed and eager to test their weapons and marksmanship on moving targets. Destruction of the oryx's fragile habitat by the overgrazing domestic stock also has contributed to the animal's decline. The days when a thousand animals or more made up a single herd are gone, and although about 10,000 members of the species still survive in scattered populations, they will not last long if the slaughter continues unchecked.

White rhinoceros | *Ceratotherium simum*

Second only to the elephant in size, the white rhinoceros runs to 3 tons or more in weight and stands 6½ feet tall. Its common name is a misnomer, for its thick hide is really gray; "white" is probably a corruption of the Dutch *wijd,* or "wide," which would adequately describe the animal's broad muzzle. For this reason, the common name preferred today is square-lipped rhinoceros. There are two races of this rhino, one in the northern grasslands of Africa and one in the south. Very similar, both are tanklike creatures with very poor eyesight but keen senses of smell and hearing. Their double horns, composed of tightly massed horny fibers, can grow to spectacular dimensions: record lengths are 62¼ inches for the southern rhino and 47¼ inches for the northern race. To a large extent, the rhino's horn has been its undoing, for despite protective legislation, the trade in horns for supposed medicinal and aphrodisiacal purposes in the Orient goes on still, costing many animals their lives. The rest of the rhino is useful, too—its meat is good to eat, and its tough hide was

once prized for making shields and whips. As a result of overhunting, the southern race was brought to the brink of extinction decades ago. Sound conservation measures, however, applied to a small pocket of animals surviving in Zululand, saved the race, and today it has recovered to such an extent that surplus individuals are used to stock national parks and zoos. The situation with the northern race is not as good. Formerly widespread, it exists today only in parts of the Sudan and Uganda and in the Garamba National Park in the Congo. There were about 1,000 animals in the park in 1963 when rebel soldiers from Sudan crossed the border, occupied the area, and went on a shooting spree. When they were done 900 rhinos lay dead. Estimates of the population in the Sudan and Uganda are unreliable, but it is known that a small group moved into Murchison Falls National Park in 1961 is apparently prospering. With continued human development of the rhino's habitat, the animal's sole hope for survival may rest in a series of protected national parks and refuges.

Black rhinoceros | *Diceros bicornis*

The black rhino, which also is really gray, stands about 5½ feet tall and weighs only about 1½ tons, considerably less than its square-lipped relative. Its muzzle is quite different, too, for the upper lip is pointed or hooked, distinguishing it as a browser on leaves and twigs rather than a grazer. It also has a much uglier and more aggressive temperament and has been known to charge vehicles and even campfires without provocation. The black rhino was formerly widespread in Africa's open lands from the Cape up to Ethiopia and the Sudan, and west as far as Lake Chad and Cameroon. Although heavily hunted, it is more abundant than the square-lipped rhino, with an estimated population between 11,000 and 13,500. About half this total is in Kenya and Tanzania. The animal has been declining at a rapid rate, however, and in many areas is being exterminated systematically to make room for human expansion, despite legal protection. Habitat destruction also works against the animal, and illegal hunting for that highly prized trading item,

Black rhinoceros

Hartmann's mountain zebra

Leonard Lee Rue IV/Bruce Coleman Inc.

rhino horn, is a constant threat that has never been satisfactorily controlled. As with the square-lipped rhinoceros, the best hope for the black rhino seems to be in reserves, where poaching can be kept to a minimum.

Cape mountain zebra | *Equus zebra zebra*
Hartmann's mountain zebra | *E. z. hartmannae*
As their name suggests, these zebras are specialized mountain animals capable of clambering about in steep, rocky canyons to obtain food and water. The Cape race, the first zebra seen by Europeans, is the smallest of the zebra family, about 48 inches at the shoulder, and has always been restricted, so far as is known, to the mountains of Cape Province. It has narrow stripes everywhere except on the rump, where they broaden out, and a dewlap under the chin, and in general outline looks more like a donkey than other zebras. Hartmann's animal is larger, about 51 inches, its stripes are wider, with the pale ones sometimes broader than the black, and the legs are usually banded equally in black and buff. This zebra lives in the mountain ranges along the Namib Desert and in the desert itself, and in former times ranged down to the coast.

The Cape zebra, probably never numerous, went into decline with the arrival of white settlers. Hunters took a steady toll; the expansion of farming activities and sheep-raising squeezed the animals off the best parts of their former range. By 1937, the year the Mountain Zebra National Park was belatedly established in South Africa, only 45 animals were left, all of them on private farms. The first 6 animals placed in the park did not multiply—only one was a mare—but in later years new stock was added and the park was expanded, and today there are some 70 Cape mountain zebra there, plus several small herds on farms in the mountains.

Hartmann's mountain zebras are in a much healthier state at the moment—an estimated 5,000 to 8,000 animals are in the range—but the total has dropped considerably in recent years and the subspecies seems to be on the downward slide. Blame for the decline has been put on "game-proof" veterinary fences, which, stretching for miles, prevent seasonal movements by the animals and sometimes cut them off from water. Conservationists are calling for corrective measures before it is too late—as it almost was for the Cape mountain zebra.

Endangered Birds

Dappled bulbul | *Phyllastrephus orostructus*
Named for the unusual olive green spots on its pale yellow breast, the dappled bulbul was first discovered by ornithologists on an expedition to Namuli Mountain in northern Mozambique in 1932. In 1935, another specimen, more brightly colored, was collected in the Amani Forest in the Usambara Mountains of Tanzania, seven hundred miles farther to the north. Since then, the Namuli bird has not been seen again, and watchers for the Usambara type had to wait until 1965 before 4 more were found. The dappled bulbul makes the endangered list not necessarily because it is in danger of extinction (although it may be, since so little is known about it), but because it is so rare.

West African ostrich | *Struthio camelus spatzi*
The largest of living birds, flightless ostriches were found in historical times in large numbers throughout the dry savanna and sandy wastelands of Africa and southwest Asia, and in ages past ranged into southern Europe and as far north and east as Mongolia. Today, the ostrich, or camel bird, is now common in the wild only in East Africa. In South Africa, where the bird was almost exterminated for its feathers, large ostrich farms maintain a considerable number, a more sensible way by far of harvesting feathers. And there are now feral ostriches in Australia, where domesticated birds were introduced some years ago and escaped into the wild. But in most other areas the ostrich is extinct or so reduced in numbers as to be approaching that unhappy status. The West African ostrich, the camel bird of the Rio de Oro region of the Spanish Sahara, is gone or almost gone, a victim of human predation.

West African ostrich

Grey-necked rock fowl | *Picathartes oreas*
White-necked rock fowl | *Picathartes gymnocephalus*

Little is known about these rare birds, known as bare-headed rock fowl and distinguished by the color of the skin on their bald heads. They are West African forest inhabitants, the white-necked from Togo, Sierra Leone, and Ghana, the grey-necked from Cameroon. They are in trouble from two factors—destruction of their forest habitat and the relentless pursuit of the trade in rare and unusual birds.

Teita olive thrush | *Turdus helleri*

A subspecies of the olive thrush, this black-headed bird with olive back brushed with rust, and a white front is known only from the remaining forest on Kenya's Teita Hills, a total of no more than one thousand acres of habitat. It has been seen only rarely—2 or 3 in one area in 1953 and 8 in another area in 1965. Outside this range, one bird was seen on Kilimanjaro and ornithologists are hoping it also breeds there, since the Teita Hills are outside Tsavo National Park and the forested area may disappear in the future.

Dappled bulbul

Teita olive thrush

Grey-necked rock fowl

Philip Jones

Prince Ruspoli's turaco

Prince Ruspoli's turaco | *Tauraco ruspolii*
This striking pigeon-size bird with iridescent green, blue, and reddish purple plumage is one of twenty species of beautiful birds occurring in Africa south of the Sahara in any kind of habitat containing trees. It is sometimes known as the loury or plantain-eater, but the last is a misnomer, for although it consumes most fruits readily, in the wild it does not, for some reason, eat bananas. Perhaps the most remarkable thing about turacos is the fact that their brilliant coloration comes not from refraction in the feather structure, but from certain pigments in the feathers that are unique in the bird world. Prince Ruspoli's turaco is rare and limited to a habitat of about ten square miles of juniper and evergreen growth in the Ethiopian highlands, a combination of factors that puts it in jeopardy. It is also reported that, when a bird species becomes rare in some areas of Africa, parts of its body are highly prized by tribal peoples for "medicinal," decorative, and other purposes—just one more hazard for creatures with problems enough.

127

Endangered Reptiles

Nile crocodile | *Crocodylus niloticus*
The Nile crocodile once was abundant all along the Nile River, throughout the rest of Africa south of the Sahara, and on Madagascar and the Seychelles Islands. A large species, it is said to have attained a length of 33 feet in the past, a possibility for very old individuals, since crocodiles continue to grow all their lives. Nowadays, however, it is difficult to find specimens longer than 20 feet. The ancient

Nile crocodile

Bruce Coleman Inc.

Egyptians, fearing the great crocodile for its ferocity, worshiped it and protected it from hunting in spite of its reputation for killing humans. Today, with few swampy areas along the Nile not settled by humans, the crocodile has just about disappeared in Egypt. Elsewhere in its range, poachers have caused a drastic decline in numbers, especially in the last twenty years. Pressure from baboons, monitor lizards, honey badgers, marabou storks, and other creatures preying on eggs and hatchlings contribute to the decline, and the Nile crocodile is now at the point of extinction in many parts of its African range.

ASIA
Creation on a Breathtaking Scale

John Tveten

The supercontinent of Eurasia is the largest land mass on earth. Take Europe away and the area that's left, Asia, is still the largest land mass on earth. Asia takes its name from the ancient Assyrian *asu,* which means "land of the East," but it is so vast a land that a phrase such as "the East" is inadequate to describe it.

In the north Asia extends far above the Arctic Circle in a broad band and reaches out almost to touch Alaska. In the south the tip of India nearly penetrates the Equator, and the islands of the southeast, bulging below that mid-globe belt, are like stepping stones to New Guinea and Australia. The eastern coast is washed from top to bottom by the northern Pacific. The western boundary stops at the Urals and European Russia, but bellies out in the southwest to reach the Mediterranean, the Suez Canal, and the Red Sea.

This enormous expanse of land—and rivers, lakes, and seas—provides every conceivable sort of environment. Great horizontal bands of boggy tundra and taiga, the largest evergreen forest in the world, march southward to the steppes, an almost treeless corridor of grasslands extending from China and the Russian river basins into eastern Europe. South of the steppes come the cold deserts of the interior, the immense Gobi and Takla Makan, which stretch from central China in a largely uninterrupted belt of wasteland to join with the Sahara in Africa. South of the deserts, the Himalayas, highest and most spectacular mountain range in the world, rear the massive wall that separates central and northern Asia from India and the lands of the southeast. Here a new and different world begins, a world of hot, humid climate and dense rain forests. Here too are monsoon forests, composed of deciduous trees that lose their leaves to the dry season.

Each of this variety of environments has its unique forms of animal life, and in sum they are as diverse in their way as Africa's, and equally endangered. From the Siberian tiger, elk, and deer in the north to the Arabian oryx in the Middle East and the monkey-eating eagle in the Philippines, all are in retreat as human populations swell and human activities reach into the most remote fastnesses.

Cheetah

Preceding pages:
Great Indian rhinoceros
Gladys Porter Zoo

Endangered Mammals

Anoa | *Anoa depressicornis*

There are two or three subspecies of anoa, depending upon which source you read, all native to the Celebes in Indonesia. For the sake of convenience, assume two—a highland race and a lowland race. They are the smallest wild cattle in the world, the lowland anoa standing only about 3 feet at the shoulder and the highland between 2 and 2½ feet. Both are sturdy, with blocky bodies and short legs, and their color ranges from dark brown to black, with many adults virtually hairless. Horns are almost straight and up to 15 inches long. Before World War II the lowland anoa was rarely hunted by primitively armed tribesmen, even though its flesh is considered excellent, because of its vicious temper. It existed in relative abundance, therefore, although it was pushed back from the coast by expanding human occupation. As an aftermath of the war, however, modern firearms became common, and hunting the lowland anoa with a rifle took less courage than tackling one with a spear. This fact, plus the breakdown of the system of nature reserves and game laws formerly enforced by the Dutch, resulted in an unbelievable slaughter of the animal. The anoa of the mountain regions, less fierce and therefore long hunted with spear and dog, may have fared somewhat better because of the difficult terrain it occupies. But both races are in perilous condition, the lowland anoa virtually exterminated and the highland not far behind.

Asia wild ass | *Equus hemionus*

There are, or were, five races of wild asses widely distributed throughout Asia in former times: the Syrian wild ass, the Persian wild ass, or onager, the Mongolian wild ass, or kulan, the Indian wild ass, and the kiang of Tibet and the Himalayas. The first mentioned, the Syrian race, which roamed over a large area of the Middle East, has not been seen since 1927 and is considered to be extinct. The kiang, with a shoulder height of 54 inches, is the tallest of the wild asses. Its coat is a pale chestnut in summer, more reddish in winter. It is rare in its range in Tibet but not yet seriously endangered. The plight of the Indian ass, sandy in color and about 4 feet tall at the shoulders, is somewhat worse, as there are now only about 800 to 900 animals, mostly in the Little Rann of Kutch, where they are protected by the vegetarian preferences of the people, plus a few in southern Sind. The kulan, about 50 inches at the shoulder and reddish brown in color, is seriously threatened, surviving today in small numbers only in the south of the Mongolian People's Republic and over the frontier in China. Because of their speed and stamina— they have been clocked at 44 miles an hour for 6 miles, and can maintain a pace of 25 to 30 miles an hour almost indefinitely—kulans were able to withstand hunting for their highly prized flesh and hides until the aftermath of World War II brought modern firearms into play. But

San Diego Zoo

Anoa

there are no animals faster than speeding bullets pumped out by repeating rifles. The onager, by tradition the animal that carried Jesus into Jerusalem on Palm Sunday, is smaller and slighter than the other wild asses of Asia but is nevertheless known also for its speed and endurance. Captured as foals and trained, these animals were esteemed as riding asses in Persia and Arabia. They were also hunted for their meat, and in Persia their bile was long supposed to be a remedy for dim vision and cataracts. Formerly they ranged across the southern part of Russia, Turkmenia, Afghanistan, and Iran. Today, in serious trouble, they can be found in Russia only in the Badkhyz Reserve, where the population has stabilized at about 700 animals, on an island game reserve in the Aral Sea, and in isolated areas of Iran.

Banteng | *Bos javanicus*

A species of wild ox found in southeast Asia, the banteng is related to the gaur, the largest wild ox on earth, but is slightly smaller (5½ feet at the shoulder) even though it has longer legs. Bantengs are found in several races from Burma through Thailand and into the northern part of the Malay Archipelago, ranging in color from shining blue black to tawny. They are upland forest animals in the monsoon season, feeding on bamboo shoots, but in the dry season they return to the grassy valleys. On Bali and Java they have been domesticated, and on the latter island fewer than 300 survive in the wild.

Wild Asiatic buffalo | *Bubalus bubalis*

The domesticated buffalo is common throughout most of southern Asia, but the larger,

San Diego Zoo

Banteng

Asia wild ass

Holy Land Conservation Fund, Inc.

fiercely aggressive wild buffalo survives now only in two areas in India and one in Nepal, near the border. This massive animal stands almost 6 feet at the shoulder, with huge, back-sweeping horns that measure up to 78 inches long, the record. Its preferred habitat is open grassland near water, the same kind of region that attracts settlers. Many animals have been killed not only for their meat and hides, but on the grounds of crop protection. Heavy losses also have resulted from diseases transmitted by domestic cattle. Both India and Nepal have created buffalo sanctuaries to preserve the estimated 2,000 surviving animals.

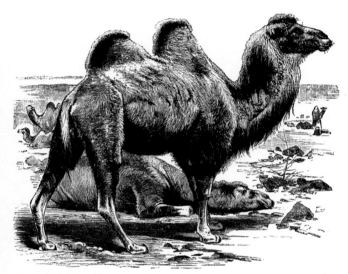

Wild Bactrian camel   Lydekker, *The Royal Natural History*

Wild Bactrian camel | *Camelus bactrianus ferus*

The wild Bactrian camel has two humps for storing food just as the domesticated animal of its species does, but it is less heavily built, less hairy, and its humps are smaller. Until the 1920s, wild camels were found throughout the Gobi area, but overhunting and increased competition from domestic stock for grazing space and water resulted in a severe drop in the population. After World War II the wild Bactrian camel was thought to be extinct, but recent research has shown that it still survives in two main groups, one in southwestern Mongolia, numbering 400 to 500, and the other, of unknown numbers, in northwestern China.

Cheetah | *Acinonyx jubatus*

Reputedly the fastest animal in the world, the cheetah has been clocked at 88 miles an hour and is said to have reached a speed of 42 mph in two seconds! Easily tamed, it has been used by humans since the days of ancient Sumer, about 3000 B.C., as a hunting helper, and is sometimes called the hunting panther. Long of leg and slender of build, cheetahs are about 7 feet long, including the tail, and weigh about 130 pounds. In some ways they are more like dogs than cats: they cannot withdraw their claws into sheaths, their feet have hard pads with sharp edges rather than soft, elastic pads, and although they can climb trees as kittens, they seem to lose the capability as they mature. There are about a dozen species of cheetahs, all with the same basic appearance—reddish yellow coat broken by spots of solid black, with dark "tear stripes" running from the eyes down the sides of the nose. They originally inhabited the dry areas of Africa and Asia, from Morocco and Algeria to the Transvaal, into Egypt, Ethiopia, Arabia, Persia, and India. Today the range is pretty much the same, but the numbers have fallen off, especially in Asia. The African cheetahs are still fairly numerous, at least in some areas, such as the Serengeti National Park, but the Asiatic races can be found only in small numbers in Iran and parts of the USSR, where they are fully protected.

Otter civet | *Cynogale bennetti*

Like the otter in appearance and its preference for water, this civet of Borneo and Sumatra measures almost 3 feet in length and weighs about 9 pounds. Its short coat is light chestnut, its whiskers long and thick, and its toes are webbed for swimming, although it is a good climber, too. It eats water creatures, birds, small mammals, and vegetation.

Eld's brown-antlered deer | *Cervus eldi*

The Indian race of this swamp deer of Southeast Asia, limited to a 7,000-acre reserve on the southern shore of Logtak Lake in the state of Manipur, is the most threatened of the animal's three subspecies. Standing 4 feet at the shoulder, males are dark brown in winter and chestnut in summer; females are a

Wild Asiatic buffalo

Otter civet

consistent reddish fawn. Both sexes have hooves specially adapted for moving about in their mushy habitat. In times of high flood, however, they move to drier land, where, in times past, waiting natives slaughtered them regardless of sex or age. In much earlier days, Indian princes protected the deer and cut off the hand of anyone caught poaching. British governors in the latter part of the nineteenth century rescinded this harsh penalty, and the local populations proceeded to attack the deer without mercy. Today, although Eld's brown-antlered deer has been under modern protection since 1934, only about 100 are left.

McNeill's deer | *Cervus elaphus macneilli*
The demands of China's ancient art of pharmaceutics have brought this little-known deer of the Sino-Tibet border area to the brink of extinction. In fact, as long ago as 1937 it was believed to be on the way out, and if more information were available it might well be moved from the endangered list to the ultimate list. Why has this deer been so mercilessly persecuted? Because its antler velvet is supposed to contain powerful aphrodisiac properties.

Persian fallow deer | *Dama mesopotamica*
Considerably larger and more brightly colored than the related common fallow deer of Europe, this subspecies is also spotted white on its tawny coat, but the spots blend into an unbroken line along the sides of its dark dorsal stripe. It is also distinguished by antlers that terminate in 3 tines. Well known in ancient times, when it appeared often in the art of Mesopotamia and other early civilizations, it was widely distributed over much of the Middle East and northeastern Africa. With the steady drying up of the countryside it gradually disappeared from most of its range and was not rediscovered until 1875. Less than fifty years later, after one specimen was shot in Iraq in 1917, it was considered extinct. But it was discovered once again in the 1950s, in two small areas densely overgrown with forests of poplar, tamarisk, and acacia along the Dez and Katkeh rivers in southwestern Iran. Villagers cutting into the woodlands for fuel

and domestic animals foraging for food now threaten this last resort of the 30 to 50 Persian fallow deer left in the wild, and the Iranian government has set aside several separated reserves where the animals can, hopefully, breed themselves into stronger numbers.

Swamp deer | *Cervus duvauceli*
Also known as the barasingha, the swamp deer is brown above and yellowish below, and in addition to antlers the male wears a mane. Found on the western slopes of the Himalayas in the frontier region between India and Nepal, and from Kashmir to Assam, these animals range through high swampy valleys but come down to the lower valleys in winter. It is estimated that no more than 3,500 barasinghas survive in India and Nepal, and the number is dropping steadily because of inroads on the population not only by tigers and leopards, but by human poachers.

Swamp deer　　　　　New York Public Library

Ceylon elephant | *Elephas maximus maximus*
The Asian elephant differs from its African cousin in several ways: its ears are much smaller, as are its tusks; females and some males are tuskless; its back is humped and its head is domed; in overall size it is slightly smaller—about 20 feet long and 8 feet tall at the shoulders, with a weight of 4 or 5 tons; and, perhaps most important of all, its temperament is calmer—it can be tamed. For centuries these elephants have been trained and used for work, war, and royal displays. In fact, the elephants that perform in circuses are all of the Asian race and almost invariably are females, for the males sometimes can be dangerous. Of the four races of Asian

elephants, the Ceylon elephant is considered the finest, an animal superior in strength, size, courage, and intelligence. But because they are destructive, especially to sugarcane, a favored food, they fall into the category of pests and are legally hunted. Only about 2,500 remain in the wild on the island, and unless reserves are established for them these spectacular and useful beasts may be exterminated.

Kloss gibbon | *Hylobates klossi*
Pileated gibbon | *H. pileatus*
Gibbons, found only in tropical Asia, are the smallest of the great apes and probably the most agile. They appear clumsy on the ground, for they run with their arms stretched to the side or over their heads—but if they didn't run this way the long limbs would literally drag on the ground. Up in their treetop element, however, their true gracefulness shows as they swing from branch to branch, leaping distances of 30 feet or more with ease. The name Hylobates comes from the Greek and means ''tree walker.'' One gibbon was seen to catch a bird in midleap, transfer it from hands to feet for safekeeping, and catch the next branch without missing ''stride.'' Gibbons are also known for their loud, whooping calls, which can be heard over long distances. Most of the races are about 3 feet tall, but the smallest, the Kloss gibbon, also known as the pygmy siamang, reaches only 18 inches in height. A

native of several small islands west of Sumatra, it is endangered. The pileated gibbon from Thailand, Laos, and Cambodia is extremely rare. It shows a sexual color difference—the fur is pearl gray, with chest and head patch black, but sexually mature males turn totally black except for a grayish white fringe around the crown of the head.

Pygmy hog | *Sus salvanius*
A wild pig in miniature, so small that a fully grown boar is about the size of a hare, the pygmy hog lives in the swamplands that lie at the base of the Himalayas in India, Nepal, Bhutan, and Sikkim. Following World War II, as the swamps were drained to make way for crops and grazing land, the pygmy hog lost much of its habitat and now survives in severely depleted numbers.

Przewalski's horse | *Equus przewalskii*
The last of the wild horses, this stocky animal is about the size of a pony, has a large head and a long tail, and differs from the domestic horse in its mane, which is stiff and erect. Its color ranges from yellowish brown to reddish brown to gray, with a dark stripe running down the back; the lower legs are black and often striped. These horses are named after Nikolai Przewalski, the man who discovered them in 1879 but thought they were tame Mongolian horses reverting to the wild. The zoologist Y. A. Polyakov argued that they were living fossils of

San Diego Zoo

Przewalski's horse

San Diego Zoo

Gladys Porter Zoo

Ceylon elephant

Pileated gibbon

Douc langur

142

Asiatic lion

the Ice Age, but no one believed him and no attempt was made to preserve the animals. The spread of civilization, with domestic stock competing for grazing and water, coupled with uncontrolled hunting, brought the wild horse to a precarious state. It survives today only in one area of southwestern Mongolia, near the Gobi Desert and the Chinese frontier. There are more Przewalski's horses in captivity than there are in the wild, and the Prague Zoo maintains a studbook.

Kouprey | *Bos sauveli*
Related to the banteng, the kouprey stands about 6 feet tall and is generally blackish with lighter undersides and white stockings on the legs; cows are smaller and gray to brown. Both have a dewlap between the forelegs, the bull's so long it often drags in the grass. The horns are the largest and have the widest spread of any living wild cattle other than the buffalo. Koupreys were discovered only in 1937, when their population was estimated at perhaps 800 to 1,000. Since then, with intermittent warfare in the area of their range—Cambodia and western Viet Nam—and uncontrolled hunting by both guerilla and regular soldiery, the population has dropped to about 200, in two widely separated areas of northern Cambodia along the Mekong River.

Douc langur | *Pygathrix nemaeus*
Also known as the yellow-faced douc, this is one of the most colorful of mammals, with a face that is indeed yellow, a brown head with a chestnut band below the ears, white whiskers, a brilliant red throat, a mottled gray body, a white rump and tail, black upper limbs, white forearms and chestnut lower legs—a color scheme right out of a kindergarten crayon box. Little is known about these large, leaf-eating monkeys from the tropical rain forests of Laos and Viet Nam and perhaps Hainan Island. Always rare, they apparently have been injured drastically as a viable species by habitat destruction and the lengthy war in Southeast Asia.

Pagi Island langur | *Simias concolor*
A small, upturned nose with nostrils opening toward the front and a small, almost hairless

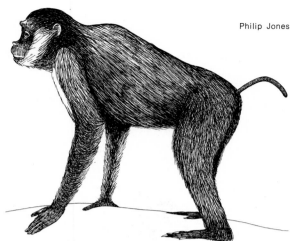

Philip Jones

Pagi Island langur

tail give this leaf-eating primate its alternate name—short-tailed snub-nosed monkey. Its short fur, ranging in tone from brown to buff, grows straight back except for tufts over the ears. These monkeys apparently have never existed in captivity, where they could be studied, and their habitat in the swamps of the islands of South Pagi, Sipora, and Siberut off Sumatra's western coast is almost impenetrable —or was, until men started draining operations.

Leopard | *Panthera pardus*
See *Barbary leopard* in Chapter 7, page 115. Mammals of Africa.

Formosan clouded leopard | *Neofelis nebulosa brachyurus*
Clouded leopards, slender, agile, tree-climbing night stalkers, range from Nepal, Sikkim, and Bhutan to Taiwan and from southeast China to Sumatra, Java, and Borneo. Like all big cats, their future is in peril because of human hunting and habitat reductions, but the Formosan race is especially endangered. This particular leopard has a somewhat shorter tail than the other subspecies, but in other respects it is similar: coat of dark gray or brown to yellow buff, fading to whitish on the under-parts, marked by large dark spots surrounded by lighter areas, which provide the clouded effect. The length ranges up to 6 feet including tail. The animal is remarkable for its extremely long canine teeth and its broad, spatulate paws, thought by some to be used as a kind of swatter when hunting birds. This is denied by

Formosan clouded leopard

other zoologists, who maintain the leopard cannot use its paws in tree hunting because it would lose its balance and fall. For centuries the Chinese have dried parts of the clouded leopard's body and used them for medicinal purposes, a fact that may help to explain the animal's decline.

Snow leopard | *Panthera uncia*
Roving the mountain ranges of Russia, Siberia, Mongolia, and western China, the snow leopard has become adapted to thin mountain air and rarely descends below 6,000 feet in summer. Generally, it inhabits the area between 10,000 and 20,000 feet, but lives at the edge of the snow-line, not in regions of year-round snow. It wears a magnificent cream to gray coat spotted with large but indefinite rosettes. Its total length is about 7 feet, including a 3-foot tail, and it looks heavier than it is because of its thick fur. This luxurious pelt obviously is highly regarded in the fur trade, and pit traps baited with young sheep have taken many snow leopards. Iron traps also are used, and a

Snow leopard

number of animals offered to zoos have been maimed by the metal teeth. Snow leopards hunt at night for mountain goats, gazelle, deer, wild boar, rabbits, ground squirrels, and birds. They, alone among the cats, have a specific breeding season, probably because of the harsh climatic conditions under which they live. Mating occurs in late winter, and after a gestation period of about 100 days the cubs, generally 2 to 4, are born just as the weather begins to warm up in the spring. Game laws are nonexistent in much of the snow leopard's range, so that the animals are becoming rare, even though they are not the easiest of targets —equipped with great strength and agility, they can clear 30 feet in a single bound and leap to a height of 10 or 12 feet.

Asiatic lion | *Panthera leo persica*
Differing little in general appearance and characteristics from the African lion, the Asiatic race was once widely distributed throughout much of Asia Minor, the Arabian peninsula, and east to India. Expanding human populations pushed the big cat into decline, not only because it raided man's livestock but because men feared for their own lives. It was common in Israel in biblical times, for example, but was exterminated there by the thirteenth century. In other areas, however, mostly remote regions, it held on until the present century. Today, the only known surviving Asiatic lions are in the Gir Forest on India's Kathiawar Peninsula, where they have been officially protected since 1900. The forest has shrunk in size over the years to about 309,000 acres and provides habitat now for little more than 100 lions, because more than 7,000 natives and possibly 60,000 domestic animals also make use of the forest area. Through overgrazing, the nearby Gir Thar Desert is advancing at a rate of one-half mile a year, and experts predict that the forest, which is basically second growth and thorn scrub, will not survive much longer than twenty years. In 1966, what was left of the forest was set aside as the Gir Wild Life Sanctuary, but was opened up again to grazing a few years ago when drought threatened to wipe out the native herds of domestic animals.

Père David's Deer: Saved

Can managed wildlife reserves really keep a species from being swallowed by the tide of extinction? The case of Père David's deer provides an illuminating example, for this animal was saved that way not once, but twice.

Père David's is in many ways a strange deer. Tawny red in summer and dull gray in its winter coat, it has a long tail and wide, splayed, reindeerlike hoofs. It sometimes grows 2 sets of antlers in the same year, and the antlers by themselves are unique, for they seem to be mounted backwards, with all the major tines protruding to the rear. So strange was this deer that the ancient Chinese, in a display of fine humor, named it *ssu-pu-hsiang,* which translates literally into "not like four." The joke goes like this: the deer is "like, yet unlike the horse; like, yet unlike the ox; like, yet unlike the deer; like, yet unlike the goat." But perhaps the most unusual thing about Père David's deer is the fact that it has never been domesticated, yet has not been seen in the wild for 3,000 years.

To understand, you have to go back to the China of antiquity, where Père David's deer was widely distributed across the plains of the northeast, living in swamps and river marshes. During the Shang dynasty, 1776–1122 B.C., the swamps were drained and put under cultivation, and the deer disappeared—except for a herd kept behind the brick wall, 45 miles in circumference, that surrounded the Imperial Hunting Park of Nan-Hai-Tsue near Peking. There the animal survived, unknown to the rest of the world, until 1865, when the noted French missionary and naturalist Abbé Armand David, ignoring the strictures against entry by Europeans, evaded the guards and scaled the park wall.

A determined man, Père David acquired a pair of skins and shipped them home, and a few years later somehow got hold of several live specimens. These too he shipped off to Europe, where they thrived. Before the end of the century, captive deer were on display in many European zoos. This was fortunate, for in 1894 raging floodwaters from the Hun Ho River crashed through the brick wall around the Imperial Hunting Park. Most of the deer that did not drown escaped into the surrounding countryside—and into the arms of the starving peasants. The survivors of that tragedy lasted until the Boxer Rebellion in 1900. when international troops stationed in the park went into the business of selling deer meat to the Chinese populace. In 1911, only 2 deer were left, and they died within the next decade.

All was not lost, however, for in England in 1900 the Duke of Bedford, disturbed by what was happening in China, managed to gather all the remaining deer from European zoos, putting them into a park at Woburn to establish a breeding herd. From this nucleus of 16 surviving animals a herd of more than 400 was built up. In the 1960s, surplus breeding stock was transferred to reserves in other countries, including China, where Père David's deer had been exterminated a half century before.

San Diego Zoo

Lion-tailed macaque

Markhor

Formosan yellow-throated marten

Lion-tailed macaque | *Macaca silenus*

Macaques are tropical and subtropical monkeys, related to the baboons but smaller and usually brown in color. The familiar rhesus, crab-eating, and pig-tailed monkeys, common in zoos and medical research facilities, belong to the macaques, which range across southern Asia from Japan and the Philippines into northern Africa. The lion-tailed macaque, black instead of the usual brown, is similar to the pig-tailed monkey and has a long white beard and mane that stand out sharply against its black fur. It is found only in the Western Ghats, a low mountain range of south India.

Markhor | *Capra falconeri*

These wild goats are noted for their spectacular spiral horns, which range from a little more than 2 feet in length in the Russian race to a huge open corkscrew of more than 5 feet in some of the specimens found on the mountain slopes of the Kashmir. They are among the largest and most powerful of the wild goats, with males standing about 3½ feet at the shoulder and weighing up to 100 pounds. Color varies from russet brown to gray tones, and old males turn almost white and grow a long beard extending down to the chest. Females are fawn-colored and about half the weight of males. The name markhor is said to be Persian for "snake eater," and natives in some areas believe that eating markhor meat will make them immune to snake venom. The animal has been avidly hunted in its mountain habitat in Iran, along the Afghanistan-Pakistan border, and into the Himalayas and Russia, and its numbers have decreased drastically. Only Russia protects the markhor, and the population there is over 1,000. Elsewhere, only small, isolated groups survive.

Formosan yellow-throated marten | *Martes flavigula chrysospila*

This is yet another creature threatened by the continuing development and expanding population of Taiwan. Perhaps the most attractive of the martens, cat-sized carnivores that are listed among the world's most valuable furbearers, it is more than 2 feet long, including its bushy tail, which makes up two-thirds of the total length. The coat is a glossy brown black, deepening to solid black on the head, neck, saddle, and legs. Shoulders and flanks are lighter, sometimes almost whitish, and the throat and chest are a bright yellow brown, tending to orange in some specimens. These martens live in high forests where they hunt both by day and by night for small vertebrates, fruit, and eggs.

Orangutan | *Pongo pygmaeus*

In Malay, orangutan means "man of the woods." The only great ape in Asia and one of the most intelligent of the primates, the orang is second in size to the gorilla: males run about 4½ feet tall, weigh up to 220 pounds, and have an armspan of 7 to 8 feet; females are considerably smaller, about 3½ feet and 75 to 100 pounds. The coat, ranging from orange to purple or blackish brown, is long and shaggy, especially over the shoulders and arms, where it may be 18 inches long. Adult males have white beards and mustaches, but most of the face is hairless, as are the hands and feet. They also have a large gular pouch and prominent cheek flanges composed of fatty tissue.

Tree dwellers for the most part, orangs build nests high up, where they sleep from dusk to dawn. They eat a wide variety of foods—seeds, plant material, and eggs—but their favorite is the durian, a pulpy, smelly fruit about the size of a football. Once widely distributed in the tropical forests of Asia, the orang can be found today only in parts of Sumatra and Borneo. Numbers have been estimated as high as 5,000 and as low as less than half that figure. The animals have been in decline since World War II primarily because timbering operations have destroyed their habitat—primary or old secondary forest in lowland areas—and have driven them back to less satisfactory mountain regions. Capturing young orangs for the zoo trade—usually by shooting the mother—also has had dire effects upon the population. This odious practice has been outlawed with legal protection of the animals, but it still goes on. Worse, because of terrible conditions in the hands of the black marketeers, an estimated 3 to 5 juvenile orangs die for every one that reaches a zoo.

Arabian oryx | *Oryx leucoryx*

Over the centuries, with its speed and endurance, the Arabian oryx was a match for camel-mounted Bedouin hunting parties, even when they were armed with guns, and managed to survive in abundance. But the combination of automobiles and repeating rifles—and airplanes, too, often enough—has been too much for this smallest species of oryx. In more recent years, fleets of vehicles, 300 and more, carrying hunters and supplies for treks lasting weeks, have invaded the *jol,* the flat plain of gravel and stone that fringes the sand desert of the Arabian peninsula. The hunters shoot everything in sight, not only oryxes but gazelles, cheetahs, and ostriches, as well. A few hundred oryxes still survive in one relatively undisturbed section of Oman, where they are under the protection of the Sultan. In addition, several small, captive breeding herds, developed as a part of Operation Oryx, which began in 1962, have been established at Riyadh in Saudi Arabia, at Slamy in Qatar, at the Hai Bar Reserve in Israel, and at zoos in Phoenix, Arizona, and Los Angeles, California.

San Diego Zoo

Arabian oryx

Giant panda | *Ailuropoda melanoleuca*

First described by the French naturalist Père David in 1869 and first seen in a zoo outside China in 1936, the giant panda looks as if it should belong to the bear family. It is, however, more closely related to raccoons, coatis, and kinkajous. Since they are so big—adults may be 6 feet long and weigh 300 pounds—and herbivorous, giant pandas spend the better part of each day chewing bamboo shoots and other fibrous material to ease their hunger. They live largely in bamboo forests in the borderland area between China and Tibet, where they are extremely rare but not necessarily in decline. They have no natural enemies other than possibly wolves and leopards, and apparently suffered their worst population setback during the 1930s, when the sudden demand by zoos and museums for specimens set off a hunting splurge among local natives. China now strictly protects the giant panda and has succeeded in breeding the animal in captivity. The World Wildlife Fund, known for its efforts to stem the tide of animal extinction, has chosen the giant panda as its symbol.

New York Public Library

Giant panda

Ryukyu rabbit   Philip Jones

Ryukyu rabbit | *Pentalagus furnessi*

The only species in its genus, this dark brown, small-eared, almost tailless rabbit occurs only on two small islands, Amami Oshima and Toku-no-Oshima, below Japan's main southern island of Kyushu. A slow breeder for a rabbit, since the doe apparently bears only a single young, it was almost wiped out by hunters in the first two decades of this century. In 1921 it was put under full protection, but deforestation and a proliferation of stray dogs on the islands kept the rabbit in a state of jeopardy. It is now almost extinct on Toku-no-Oshima, and down to fewer than 1,000—possibly as low as 500—on Amami Oshima. The animal must be protected in suitable habitat in the wild, for it has never bred in captivity.

Great Indian rhinoceros | *Rhinoceros unicornis*

Largest of the three Asiatic species, the one-horned great Indian rhino stands more than 6 feet at the shoulder, may be 14 feet long, and weighs 2 tons or more. It is built like a battleship and looks like one—loose folds in its thick hide give the appearance of armor plate, an impression enhanced by the convex tubercles that stud its sides and upper legs and resemble rivet heads. This huge animal once ranged through much of India, Nepal, and Burma, near rivers and in swamps, where it spent most of the day in the water or wallowing in mud. Even a century ago it was still plentiful enough for the government of Bengal to put a bounty of twenty rupees on its head as a wrecker of crops. Since then, however, the animal population has gone into decline as the expanding human population has taken over the lush lowlands and now even the rolling hills. Hunters have done their share to decimate the rhino, too, for the animal's horn has long had value in India as an aphrodisiac and became an even greater prize when the Javan rhino, which formerly provided horn for the China trade, was nearly exterminated. The Indian rhinoceros now can be found only in eight reserves in India and Nepal, with a total population estimated at considerably less than 1,000. Poaching and the possibility of disease from foraging domestic animals are the biggest threats to this rhinoceros today.

Javan rhinoceros | *Rhinoceros sondaicus*
Similar to the Indian species but smaller, the Javan rhino faces the same threats to its existence and in fact is several steps closer to extinction. People-pressure for space, coupled with the horn trade, has wiped out the animal all over its former range in Southeast Asia except in the Udjong Kulon Reserve at the westernmost tip of Java. Here, some two dozen rhinos still survive, down from an estimated 40 animals in 1967.

Sumatran rhinoceros | *Didermocerus sumatrensis*
Smallest of the world's rhinos and the only Asian species with two horns, the Sumatran race measures only 4½ feet at the shoulder and 8 to 9 feet in length, with a weight of about one ton. Forced out of its hillside forest habitat and hunted mercilessly for its horns (and the rest of its body, since the typical Chinese apothecary shop uses the entire animal), the Sumatran rhino is down to little over 100 animals scattered in isolated areas in Thailand, Cambodia, Borneo, Burma, and Malaya, as well as in Sumatra.

Seladang | *Bos gaurus*
This wild ox, the biggest on earth, is also known as the gaur. Bulls stand about 6 feet at the shoulder on the average (a 7-foot giant was shot in Burma some years back) and weigh as much as 2,000 pounds. The coat is usually black or brownish black, and the legs white from knees to hooves. The forehead and the arched ridge between the horns are gray white, while the horns themselves are yellowish with black tips. In males the horns turn up, but in females they bend in and sometimes cross. Gaurs live in hilly forests in India, Bangladesh, and Southeast Asia, and are seriously threatened not only by habitat destruction but by epidemics, transmitted by domestic animals, against which they apparently have little natural resistance.

Japanese serow | *Capricornis crispus*
One form of this goat antelope is restricted to Japan, the other to Taiwan. Both are smaller than the mainland serows. In Japan, the animal

Seladang

Kenneth W. Fink/Bruce Coleman Inc.

Takin

American Museum of Natural History

Wild yak

San Diego Zoo

has lost much of its forest environment, and in the past was so heavily hunted that by 1924 only a few remained. Several reserves have been established, and the population now has risen to about 1,500. In Taiwan, the serow is restricted to the more remote mountain areas, where it is still hunted for its flesh and hide and for the contributions the rest of its body can make to Chinese pharmaceutics.

Sumatran serow | *Capricornis sumatraensis sumatraensis*

In all there are eleven races of serows, medium-sized goat antelopes with long ears and smallish horns, ranging through much of southern and eastern Asia. The Sumatran serow has been forced by the continual spread of cultivation to retreat to the remote parts of the island, into the volcanic area on the western side. It has been granted nominal protection by law, but local people still hunt it for its meat and hide, using snares and dog packs. The horns are popular as charms.

Sika | *Cervus nippon*

The sika deer of eastern Asia, including Japan and Taiwan, includes a number of subspecies, most of which are endangered or possibly extinct already. Medium-sized animals, they can be as small as one of the Japanese sikas, about 25 inches at the shoulder, or as large as one of the Manchurian forms, about 43 inches. Colors range from rich chestnut red to yellow brown, liberally salted with white spots in the summer. These are basically deer of the forest, but the races that have bred in captivity adapt readily to grasslands. As with so many creatures, decline has come to the sikas through rampant habitat destruction and overhunting. The Formosan sika, almost extinct in the wild, survives in captive herds in Taiwan and other countries. Three of the Chinese races, the North China, South China, and Shansi sikas, are all on the verge of extinction or are now lost to us, driven to extremis by hunters who sought their horns for sale to the aphrodisiac market. The Ryukyu sika, given full protection in 1955, nevertheless could muster only an estimated population of 30 in recent years. Measures are being taken to provide sufficient water and forage on three small islands where they survive, and goats, competitors for food, are being removed.

Arabian tahr | *Hemitragus jayakari*
Nilgiri tahr | *H. hylocrius*

There are three species of tahrs, animals that are closely related to goats: the Himalayan, the Nilgiri, and the Arabian. The latter two are considered endangered. The Arabian tahr, the smallest, stands about 2 feet high and is slenderly built. It is sandy, with a dorsal crest, long shaggy hair, but no mane. It is limited to the mountains of Oman. The Nilgiri tahr is the biggest, 39 to 42 inches at the shoulder, and has a short yellow brown coat; old males turn dark brown with a light saddle-shaped patch on the back. Females of the Nilgiri have only one pair of teats, while the other species have 2 pairs. Nilgiri tahrs live in the mountains of southern India, with half the total population of about 800 in sanctuaries in the Nilgiri Hills. Poaching is a major problem, and one herd has already been wiped out in recent years.

Takin | *Budorcas taxicolor*

Takins are powerfully built animals related to the musk ox. They stand over 4 feet high and weigh 500 to 600 pounds. Ungainly looking, they have thick necks, short, thick legs, humped shoulders, a bulbous muzzle, and horns that turn out and then up. Color ranges from golden to dark brown, depending upon the race, of which there are three. The Mishmi takin of Assam and Bhutan is not presently considered endangered. The Szechwan and golden takins of southwestern China are both rare, especially the former, which came down to the sheltered lowlands in winter and was there persecuted by hunters until protective laws were passed by the Chinese government.

Tamaraw | *Anoa mindorensis*

The Philippines, it is said, has more guns per capita than any other country in the world. As one result of all that armament, the tamaraw, one of the smallest of the wild cattle—3½ feet at the shoulder and 600 to 700 pounds—is on the brink of extinction. This dwarf buffalo lives only on the island of Mindoro, particularly in the area of swamps and marshes, where for years malarial mosquitoes protected it from human onslaught. But with control of the mosquitoes in the 1950s, settlers moved in by the thousands to drain the swamps, clear out the forests, and force the tamaraw into even more inaccessible regions. A 100,000-acre preserve at Mount Calavite does not really protect the animals, for even here they are not safe from the guns of the hunters, some of whom use helicopters in the chase. In 1969, with the tamaraw population reduced to fewer than 100, the government finally took steps to outlaw hunting and provide meaningful sanctuary to the much-beleaguered animal.

Philip Jones

Tamaraw

Tiger | *Panthera tigris*
The tiger, which originated in Siberia and spread out over the entire continent of Asia, has seen its numbers and its range steadily reduced in historical times, solely because of its conflict with human beings. All seven surviving races are losing ground to the expansion of civilization and are under serious threat of extinction, not only because of habitat destruction but through hunting. The Chinese tiger is extremely rare and receives no protection whatsoever because it is considered a threat to human life. The Bengal tiger, found in India from the Himalayas to the south, is in less trouble than the other races, but its numbers are dwindling. The Sumatran tiger, under considerable pressure from hunters and trappers, is limited now largely to areas in the north and mountainous southwest of the island. The Javan tiger is down to only a few members in several reserves and is considered, with the Javan rhino, to be only a step from oblivion. The Bali tiger may even now be extinct,

Tiger   Lydekker, *The Royal Natural History*

possibly saved from this category only by unconfirmed counts of a few survivors in two national parks in the western part of the island. The Caspian tiger, rather small and a darker color than the others, once covered a huge area in northern Asia but is now reported only in very small numbers in Turkmenistan and Iran, and possibly larger numbers in northern Afghanistan, where no estimate has ever been made. The long-haired Siberian tiger, largest of all with a length of 13 feet and a weight of 600 pounds, is estimated to be about 100 in number in Russia, between 40 and 50 in northern Korea, and a like number in Manchuria.

Wild yak | *Bos grunniens mutus*
The largest animal of the Tibetan uplands and plateaus, the wild yak is distinguished by its long, fringed coat, which sometimes sweeps the ground. Wild yaks are always black and are considerably larger than domestic yaks, which range in color from black or brown to white and piebald. Wild yaks also have larger horns, which turn in at the tips instead of out. Discovered only about a century ago, wild yaks were found all over the Tibetan plateau and entered India through valley passes. Domestic yaks are still plentiful, but the wild creature has been on the decline in recent decades and appears to be on its way out.

Endangered Birds

Short-tailed albatross | *Diomedea albatrus*
This large white bird with dark wings and a wingspread that spans 7 feet is now considered one of the rarest birds in the world, yet it once ranged far and wide over the northern Pacific.

Short-tailed albatross

Great Indian bustard

Japanese crane

Monkey-eating eagle

Today, its last stronghold is on Torishima, one of Japan's Seven Islands of Izu, and even there it has been preyed on so heartlessly that it was recorded as extinct in the 1940s. The record of the bird's trials and tribulations reads like a horror story. From 1887, when the island was first settled, to 1903, Asian fowlers and feather hunters slew more than 500,000 birds and their young. That record stops in 1903 because a violent volcanic eruption that year killed all the hunters. But more came after the lava and ash cooled and the birds began nesting again, and by the end of 1933, when the island was declared a sanctuary, there were fewer than 100 birds left. More volcanic disturbances were assumed to have obliterated this remainder during the next decade, for in the late 1940s, after the war, no birds were seen. They were reported again in the early 1950s, however, and the population has fluctuated between 20 and perhaps 50 ever since, held down by new volcanic eruptions and raids on hatchlings by Steller's sea eagles.

Great Indian bustard | *Choriotis nigriceps*
Some of the largest flying birds in the world are the bustards, and the great Indian

154

Arabian ostrich

bustard, with a record weight of 40 pounds, ranks near the biggest of these. This great size is no favor in modern times, however, for a breeding pair needs a large territory in which to live, and large territories of grassy plains and open wastelands are hard to come by these days in the crowded Indian subcontinent. Even worse, perhaps, is the fact that the size of these birds makes them easily spotted targets for all sorts of hunters and trappers. Especially vulnerable are the males during the breeding season, as they strut about the unobtrusively nesting female, aggressively looking for enemies. Although the bustard is protected throughout its range in India, the law is not always enforced or enforceable. Since 1938 the bird has been reduced steadily in numbers and in breeding areas, and the establishment of well-protected parks and preserves seems to be the only antidote to eventual extinction.

Hooded crane | Grus monachus
Japanese crane | G. japonensis
Siberian white crane | G. leucogeranus

The rare and beautiful Japanese, or Manchurian, crane stands about 3½ feet tall on long legs. It has a pure white body with black wings, a red crown and broad gray stripes running from the sides of the head down the neck. Much reduced in range, it still breeds in a valley of the Amur River in Manchuria and in Kuccharo Marsh, a national refuge since 1925, on the Japanese island of Hokkaido. Centuries ago in Japan the bird was stringently protected and even bred by the noble class. With the Meiji restoration in 1867, however, these niceties became a thing of the past and hunters brought the bird population tumbling down. Protective laws finally were passed, and in 1925 the Japanese government designated the crane a national monument. Today, the population has risen slowly to several hundred, most of which winter in Japan, where they are strictly protected. Another 150 or so are in captivity, where they have bred reasonably well. Two other large cranes of eastern Asia, the hooded crane of swamps and marshlands and the Siberian white crane of the steppes and tundra, have been greatly depleted in numbers through hunting and habitat destruction.

Monkey-eating eagle | Pithecophaga jefferyi

The fierce monkey-eating eagle, one of the largest and most spectacular birds in Asia as well as one of the most formidable birds of prey in the world, is a native of the larger Philippine Islands. It lives in dense rain forests, nesting high above the forest canopy, often in giant kapok trees, where it preys on monkeys, flying lemurs, squirrels, and other small mammals. It also occasionally raids farms and backwoods villages, swooping down on pigs and dogs, and so has earned the enmity of man. But an angry farmer or villager with a gun is only one danger the monkey-eating eagle must face. For years, trapping these huge birds for animal dealers and zoos was a profitable trade in the Philippines, and only lately have there been efforts to put a stop to it. But now a new threat has arisen—a fad among Filipino collectors of curiosities to display mounted eagles, trophies made more prestigious, perversely enough, by the knowledge that the bird is close to extinction. Add to this the continued destruction of the eagle's habitat as Filipino farmers and lumbermen raze the great green forests, and you have a complete case history of why the bird is close to oblivion. Now confined to the surviving primeval forest on Mindanao, and possibly to small areas of Luzon and Samar, the total population is at most 100 birds and may well be below 50. Since it lays only one egg a year and has never bred in captivity, and since little is being done in the Philippines to preserve it, the monkey-eating eagle may have only a short future.

Chinese egret | Egretta eulophotes

A white, crested bird with yellow bill and feet and dark legs, the Chinese egret once ranged far and wide in Asia, from the maritime provinces of Russia and Korea through coastal China to Sarawak, the Celebes, and the Philippines. Its breeding headquarters were in Korea and the coastal wetlands of China; a small colony survives in the former, and there may still be nesting sites in China, but information coming from that vast land is scanty. It is believed that the Chinese egret is a victim—hopefully, the last—of the plume trade, which reached its zenith earlier in the century and has not yet been laid to rest.

Giant ibis | *Thaumatibis gigantea*
Japanese crested ibis | *Nipponia nippon*
The Japanese crested ibis, a medium-sized white bird with a red face and a long, slender, down-curving bill of black, once nested over a huge area that included parts of Russia, Manchuria, China, and Japan, and ranged even farther in its migratory flights. Today, only one tiny colony is known to exist, on the island of Sado in the Sea of Japan off Honshu's west coast. The decline of this bird is a familiar story: human exploitation coupled with despoilation of wooded wetlands. The giant ibis has also suffered from a reduced and disturbed habitat in the wetlands of Cambodia, Thailand, and Laos that are drained by the Mekong River and its tributaries. A shy and rare bird with a total population of only a few hundred, it is now largely limited to Cambodia and may become one of the ultimate victims of political strife and unrest in Southeast Asia.

Red-faced malkoha | *Phaenicophaeus pyrrhocephalus*
Combining a red face with shades of green and blue on its upper parts, white below, and long tail feathers of green edged with white, this strong-billed member of the cuckoo family is a colorful resident of the forests of Ceylon. It is apparently limited to that island, and its habitat has been drastically reduced as the woodlands have fallen to human settlement and agriculture. In a parallel movement, the bird population has fallen to a low level and is limited to a few stretches of surviving dense forest in two provinces. Unlike some cuckoos, this species makes its own nest and hatches its own eggs.

Arabian ostrich | *Struthio camelus syriacus*
Like the West Africa ostrich, the Arabian race is a prime candidate for extinction, if, indeed, it is not already there. The last one reported was a specimen killed and eaten by Arabs in Saudi Arabia in the vicinity of Bahrain Island. If it survives, this ostrich is a very rare bird in the wastes of southern Saudi Arabia and perhaps in Jordan. It formerly ranged over much of the Middle East, usually in company with herds of antelope and oryx, also pitifully scarce now.

Bar-tailed pheasant | *Syrmaticus humiae*
Two races of this long-tailed pheasant live in the forests of southern Asia, one ranging from eastern India to the right bank of the Irrawaddy in Burma, and the other from the left bank of the river into southwest China and northern Thailand. These birds are rare, and may be adversely affected by hunting and trapping.

San Diego Zoo

Bar-tailed pheasant

Brown-eared pheasant

Philip Jones

157

Blyth's tragopan pheasant | *Tragopan blythi*
Extremely rare, the two races of this horned bird (*tragopan* combines the Greek for goat and Pan) live in the montane forests of Burma, parts of China, and perhaps still in southeastern Tibet. They were successfully bred in captivity starting in 1884. But in later years, suffering from the lack of replenishment from the wild, the captive birds have nearly died out.

Brown-eared pheasant | *Crossoptilon mantchuricum*
No specimens of this bird of northern China's highlands have been recorded since 1949, and it may be nearing extinction. Happily, however, a captive breeding population of more than 100 is thriving in North American and European zoos.

Cabot's tragopan pheasant | *Tragopan caboti*
Destruction of the forests in China's Fukien and Kwangtung provinces, coupled with unregulated hunting, has reduced this already rare bird. In 1965, the last one trapped in China was sent out through Hong Kong to the Ornamental Pheasant Trust in Norfolk, England, where aviculturist Philip Wayre has been developing breeding stock for transplanting in the wild.

Chinese monal pheasant | *Lophophorus lhuysi*
This species, extremely rare, has never bred in captivity. A bird of the high coniferous forests and alpine meadows, it has been severely persecuted by hunters and probably survives now, if at all, only in China's Szechwan Province.

Edward's pheasant | *Lophura edwardsi*
The missionary Père Renauld discovered this bird in 1895 in the interior of Viet Nam, and the four skins he obtained were the only record until a French expedition under Jean Delacour and Pierre Jabouille brought back 22 live birds in 1924. These birds provided the nucleus for the ''flock'' of more than 200 now in captivity in Western zoos.

Elliot's pheasant | *Syrmaticus ellioti*
This beautiful long-tailed pheasant travels pretty much the same range as Cabot's tragopan, in China's eastern provinces below the Yangtze River, and is losing ground in the face of increasing forest destruction in the mountains. It was also victimized by plumage hunters until its numbers became too few to make the effort worthwhile. The captive population, however, is in good shape—more than 350 birds.

Imperial pheasant | *Lophura imperialis*
Discovered in 1923 by the same expedition that captured the first live Edward's pheasants, the imperial bird inhabited a heavily forested area near the Viet Nam-Laos border where humans were few, a fact that certainly worked to the bird's advantage. Progeny from the pair sent back to France by the Delacour-Jabouille expedition now total about 25, but inbreeding has weakened the stock.

Mikado pheasant | *Syrmaticus mikado*
A mountain bird of Taiwan, the mikado pheasant has been hunted down to a population of only a few hundred. But the future looks brighter for this most handsome of the long-tailed pheasants, for the government of Taiwan is developing a reserve for the birds, and young are being bred in captivity for release into the wild.

Palawan peacock pheasant | *Polyplectron emphanum*
A victim of the juggernaut that the Philippine logging industry has become since World War II, the Palawan peacock pheasant, a beautiful and dainty bird with colorful plumage in intricate designs, is nowhere common in its former range on the outlying island of Palawan. More than 100 birds are in captivity to form the nucleus of a zoo bank, but they breed slowly and not easily, and an appropriate natural reserve on the island, to which they may eventually be transplanted, has not yet been set aside.

Sclater's monal pheasant | *Lophophorus sclateri*
This mountain bird is still listed as possibly

existing in Burma, China, India, and perhaps near the Himalayas in Tibet. It has not been seen in the wild since 1938, however, and the only one known to have been taken into captivity arrived at the London Zoo in 1870 and eventually died there.

Swinhoe's pheasant | *Lophura swinhoei*

Although more than a century has passed since the discovery of this bird in 1862, the extent of its range is still unknown, largely because of its rarity. It seems certain, however, that rapid human growth and consequent land development on Taiwan have adversely affected this pheasant. Naturalists believe that the captive population, estimated at 600 a few years ago, is very likely larger than the wild population. In 1967 the Ornamental Pheasant Trust, based in England, sent 15 pairs of Swinhoe's pheasants to Taiwan for release in the Experimental Forest of the University of Taipei at Hsitou.

Western tragopan pheasant | *Tragopan melanocephalus*

Nothing has been heard of this rare pheasant since 1939, when 2 captive pairs were displayed in Bombay. Its former range was in the Swat and Kashmir areas of Pakistan and India, where it lived in temperate forests. It was first bred successfully in 1894, but all captive specimens in Western collections disappeared by the turn of the century.

White eared pheasant | *Crossoptilon crossoptilon*

The eared pheasants, so-named for the elongated white-feathered ear coverts common to the three species, are inhabitants of the highlands of Tibet and northwestern China. All the subspecies of the white eared pheasant, only one of which is primarily white, are rare and are under growing threat from retreating forests and human persecution. At one time the Tibetan races were protected by religious attitudes, but those scruples ended with occupation of the country by the Chinese. Only limited success has been achieved in breeding these birds in captivity.

Cebu black shama | *Copsychus niger cebuensis*

Cebu, the most densely populated island of the Philippines, has lost almost all its original forest cover. As a result, this subspecies of the black shama is on the verge of extinction, for it apparently cannot withstand the disturbance of its densely thicketed habitat and has not been able to adapt as other species of shama have to hedges, gardens, and bamboo groves. An expedition seeking the birds in 1956 found only one specimen—and collected it! A program of reforestation is being carried out in some areas of the island, but it has probably come too late for the black shama.

Rothschild's starling | *Leucopsar rothschildi*

The threat to Rothschild's starling comes not from habitat destruction but from human greed. The bird's population was stabilized in its very restricted range on the northern coast of the Indonesian island of Bali, but because of the limited nature of its realm the bird was considered rare. This knowledge brought a demand from zoological gardens and private collectors, and an ensuing rush into the area by bird trappers and agents for rare bird dealers. Now Rothschild's starling, the only bird in its genus, is not only rare but endangered. As might be expected, there are probably more in captivity today than there are in the wild.

Crested shelduck | *Tadorna cristata*

Several centuries ago this must have been a reasonably plentiful bird in the Orient, for it figured in text and art in Japanese books and Chinese tapestries. In more recent times, however, only four specimens have been recorded—one in Russia in 1877, a second in Korea in 1913, another in Korea in 1916, and a last, also in Korea, in 1924. After that the birds were seen no more and were assumed to be extinct. But in 1964 two experienced Russian bird watchers spied them again, a drake and two ducks, mixed in with a flock of harlequin ducks southwest of Vladivostok. Their description fit the crested shelduck to a tee— larger than a mallard, with pinkish bill and legs, sharply particolored in dark metallic green,

Rothschild's starling

Crested shelduck

Korea, and Japan and wintered in the southern part of its breeding range as well as in lower China. During the Tokugawa shogunate in Japan it was protected for two centuries, but near the end of the 1800s it went into a rapid decline. Today the bird is known only from two restricted areas of Japan, both of which have been named sanctuaries, where it nests in severely reduced numbers. It may also survive in the Russian breeding grounds. Since these birds find much of their food in marshes and shallow water, they are particularly susceptible to pollution; several have been found that had died from mercury poisoning.

gray, and white, the male with a crest, the female with white face and neck, black head, and black "eyeglasses." Later, a pair—perhaps from the original trio—was seen on a small lake in the same general area. So the crested shelduck may still survive in Russia, if not in Korea, China, and Japan.

White oriental stork | *Ciconia ciconia boyciana*

Also called the Korean white stork, this race is larger than the typical and well-known white stork of the West, with a larger bill, black instead of red, and red eye skin instead of black. Formerly it nested in Siberia, Manchuria,

White oriental stork   Philip Jones

160

Tristram's woodpecker

striking scarlet head and cheeks in the male is extinct on Tsushima and extremely rare, at best, in Korea.

Endangered Reptiles

Siamese crocodile | *Crocodylus siamensis*
The 13-foot-long Siamese crocodile is characterized by a raised triangular section in front of the eyes and a bony ridge between them. Once a resident of Thailand, Indochina, and the islands of Java and Borneo, it is now virtually extinct in the wild and survives only on a Thai crocodile farm, where the animals are raised for their skins—a conservation tactic that has prevented the species from being wiped out by poachers.

Komodo dragon | *Varanus komodoensis*
The Komodo dragon, largest lizard in the world, was not discovered until early in this century. It reaches a length of at least 10 to 12 feet and a weight of 360 pounds, and has no natural enemies on Komodo, Rintja, Flores, and Poeloe Padar, the four small islands off the coast of Indonesia that constitute its limited range. Nevertheless, by the early 1960s the giant monitor's total population had been reduced to only 300 or so, a few still on Flores and Rintja and the bulk on Komodo. The decrease was not caused by hunting—the lizard has been protected for decades—but by the fact that the native peoples are more efficient predators of the "dragon's" own prey, wild pigs and deer. The key to saving the Komodo dragon, therefore, rests with protecting the animals it preys on. With this end in mind, the island of Komodo has recently been declared a strict nature reserve.

Gavial | *Gavialis gangeticus*
The gavial, or gharial, is the only living member of its family, and is believed by some scientists to be a relative of an extinct family of sea crocodiles from the Jurassic period. It differs from all other crocodilians in its extremely long, thin snout, a specialized adaptation enabling the animal to swing its head sideways

Tristram's woodpecker | *Dryocopus javensis richardsi*
This rare woodpecker once bred extensively in Korea and on the island of Tsushima, but two wars and steady destruction of its forest habitat have brought it close to oblivion, despite protective laws. Large woodpeckers need a good-sized territory in which to find the grubs and insects they eat, and these are among the largest in the world—16 inches long. They also need huge old trees for their nest holes, and when they can't find a proper site they often refuse to breed. As a result of all these factors, this handsome black and white bird with a

in the water more easily to catch small fish, its usual prey. The gavial spends most of its life in the water, climbing out only to lay its eggs on a riverbank, and poses no special threat to humans despite its large size—up to 20 feet in length. When the gavial's mouth is closed, its teeth are locked between each other and point out at an angle. During the breeding season, the male develops a hump on the end of its snout, the only known secondary sexual characteristic in crocodiles. The gavial was formerly abundant in the Indian subcontinent, but its numbers have diminished to a dangerous level in recent years.

Komodo dragon

Siamese crocodile

Gavial

163

AUSTRALASIA
Nature's Early Experiments Preserved

The world's largest island and smallest continent, Australia is about the size of the United States, minus Alaska, and lies entirely in the Southern Hemisphere. It offers two kinds of climate: tropical in the northern third of the land, where thick evergreen forests are nourished by heavy rains in the wet season, and more temperate in the southern two-thirds. The heartland of the continent, however, is composed of forbidding deserts of sand, stone, and clay, for the Great Dividing Range that parallels the east coast, even though low and eroded with age, traps the moisture-laden clouds coming in from the Pacific and drains them of water. West of the mountain wall begin the vast stretches of arid and semi-arid lands that are under the influence of dry Antarctic air. In these inhospitable regions, many of which receive less than one inch of rain a year, it is not uncommon for temperatures to soar to a searing 120 degrees Fahrenheit during the day and plunge below the freezing point at night.

If the evidence provided by the *Nothofagus* beech is true, Australasia and Antarctica were once linked by land to South America in a great southern continent; the tree grows today in Tasmania, New Zealand, and southeast Australia as well as in South America, and traces of it have been found in the Antarctic. But that was at least 50 million years ago, and in the intervening ages of splendid geographic isolation Australia has developed its own menagerie of unusual animal life, the best known of which are the marsupials, or "pouched" mammals, a primitive form that was replaced everywhere else in the world by placental creatures—except, interestingly enough, in South America, where vestigial traces remain.

Like Australia, New Zealand has long been isolated from the rest of the world; and it has been separated from the continent of Australia for perhaps 190 million years. Lying in the Pacific more than 1,000 miles southeast of the island continent, it is a land of oceanic climate, active volcanoes, lush forests, lakes and grasslands, the towering Southern Alps, a range harboring large glaciers, and steep fiords reminiscent of Scandinavia.

Except for two species of bats, New Zealand has no native mammals—it entered its lengthy period of isolation so long ago that mammals had not yet developed. It was the home of an abundant family of huge, flightless birds, however, that apparently adapted to take advantage of the grasslands, where they grazed much like sheep and cattle. It also has preserved over the millennia a relict reptile, the tuatara, which had vanished from the rest of the world more than 135 million years ago.

John Markham/Bruce Coleman Inc.

Splendid parakeet

Preceding pages:
Yellow-footed rock wallaby
Australian Information Service Photograph by D. McNaughton

Leadbeater's possum
Australian News and Information Bureau by Gary C. Lewis

Endangered Mammals

Bandicoots

Bandicoots are rabbit-sized marsupials with pointed ears and tapering snouts. The name originally was applied to large rodents of southern Asia; in the Telugu tongue of India it means "pig rat." Australia's bandicoots have a superficial similarity to rats, but they have the same foot structure as the kangaroos and wallabies, with the hind legs enlarged to carry most of the body weight while the forelegs are used mainly for digging and scratching. They eat insects and small creatures, and some species have earned a bad name by digging up lawns in search of food.

Barred bandicoot | *Perameles bougainville*
This smallest of the barred bandicoots is also called the little marl, a native name, and is found in western Australia on Peron Peninsula and the islands in Sharks Bay. Its rarity may be the fault of introduced cats.

Desert bandicoot | *Perameles eremiana*
A dull orange color on its back gives this desert dweller an alternate name—orange-backed bandicoot. Once plentiful, it was eaten by miners at the Granites goldfield, about 200 miles northwest of Alice Springs. It is a nocturnal animal and scoops out a shallow hole to lie in during the day, thatching it over with grass. Australian natives catch it by stepping on the thatched roof and pinning the creature down.

Pig-footed bandicoot | *Chaeropus ecaudatus*
This bandicoot gets its name from the cleft or hooflike appearance of its forefeet, which apparently are an adaptation to running rather than hopping. Only a few nonnatives have seen this creature in the wild, for it fled before the tide of settlers and may even now be extinct.

Rabbit bandicoot | *Macrotis lagotis*
Lesser rabbit bandicoot | *M. leucura*
Known also as bilbies, these little animals are considered the most beautiful of Australian marsupials and are distinguished from other bandicoots by their long, silky, blue gray fur

Vogt and Specht, *The Mammalia*

Pig-footed bandicoot

Rabbit bandicoot   Philip Jones

and long, rabbitlike ears. They also are the only bandicoots to excavate an actual burrow for daytime resting, and they are expert tunnelers. The rabbit bandicoot is represented by several subspecies, all the general size of a full-grown rabbit and inhabiting most of the southern half of the country, from the coast of western Australia to the Great Dividing Range in the east. The lesser rabbit bandicoots are both dark and light in color, the former inhabiting the Charlotte Waters region north of the south Australian border, and the latter from the Lake Eyre basin. Early settlers were generally appreciative of the way these creatures preyed on insects and rodents and sometimes kept them as house pets. Later generations, however, killed many for their silky pelts or for "sport." Others were the victims of rabbit traps, poisoned bait, and the introduced fox. Today, they have retreated from the advance of civilization and can be found in reduced numbers only in the remoter, less hospitable regions, where paucity of food and water has apparently reduced the rate of their breeding.

Dibbler | *Antechinus apicalis*
Named by Australian aborigines around Perth, the Moore River, and King George's Sound, the little speckled marsupial mouse was believed to be extinct. But after eighty-three years it was found again in 1967, in the Mount Manypeaks Range, climbing "and feeding . . . upon pollen and nectar from around the spikes of Banksia flowers, and on the attracted insects" (Ellis Troughton, *Furred Animals of Australia*).

Tasmanian forrester | *Macropus giganteus tasmaniensis*
The only large kangaroo occurring in Tasmania, this animal is somewhat heavier than the mainland forrester, with longer and coarser fur of a more reddish brown tone and with larger teeth. It once ranged almost the whole of the island of Tasmania, but was hunted to the brink of extinction. It is fully protected now, and naturalists hope that it will be able to reestablish itself.

Eastern jerboa marsupial | *Antechinomys laniger*
Little is known about this tiny marsupial mouse with long, kangaroolike hind legs, large ears, and a long tail. It eats insects, small lizards, and mice. Its pouch is primitive—backward-opening instead of forward. It has been found in northwestern Victoria, New South Wales, and Queensland, but is extremely rare.

Large desert marsupial mouse | *Sminthopsis psammophila*
Long-tailed marsupial mouse | *S. longicaudatus*
These are little-known creatures, described by zoologists from just a few specimens. The large desert marsupial mouse is characterized by its size, biggest of its genus, its expansive ears, and its slender tail. It has been found near Lake Amadeus in central Australia. The long-tailed form comes from the arid regions of western Australia and is distinguished by its remarkably long tail, twice the length of the animal's body.

Australian Information Service Photograph

Dibbler

169

Tasmanian forrester

Field mouse *(Alice Springs pseudo rat)* | *Pseudomys fieldi*

Apparently known erroneously in some places outside Australia as the "field mouse," this extremely rare animal was named after J. Field in recognition of his valuable service to the Horn Expedition to Central Australia some years ago. Obviously the creature is not very well known.

Gould's eastern mouse | *Pseudomys gouldii*

How rare is rare? This species, described as being intermediate in size between a mouse and a rat, buffy brown above and paler below, with long, slender white feet, has not been recorded since the early days of its discovery more than 100 years ago in northeastern New South Wales. It has not been added to the list of extinct creatures only because of a belief that it may still survive in areas where it might be thought of as "just another rat."

New Holland mouse | *Pseudomys novaehollandiae*

This is another rare creature of northeastern New South Wales that has not been recorded since the early days of settlement, when it was fairly common on the plains and stony ridges, where it often hid in ground fissures and under rocks. It is similar to the ordinary house mouse, which may explain why it cannot be readily identified.

Sharks Bay mouse | *Pseudomys praeconis*

A loose blue gray coat earns this species its alternate name, shaggy mouse. It is distinguished from other western forms in its genus by its very long bicolored tail, brown or black above and white below. It was found on Peron Peninsula in Western Australia, but was considered extinct on the mainland as early as 1906. It may survive on Bernier Island.

Shortridge's mouse | *Pseudomys shortridgei*

This medium-sized species from southwestern Australia is also known as the western pseudo rat. It was originally trapped in swampy country surrounded by thick brush.

Smoky mouse | *Pseudomys fumeus*

Only 4 specimens of this mouse are known. They were all collected in one locality in the Cape Otway Ranges of southern Victoria. Relatively large at 4½ inches, excluding the shortish tail, this mouse is smoky gray in color; hence its name.

Smoky mouse

Eastern native-cat | *Dasyurus viverrinus*

This predatory marsupial, about the size and general shape of a domestic cat, is similar to the spotted tiger but smaller, and lacks spots on the tail. It once ranged New South Wales, Victoria, South Australia, and Tasmania, at home near human settlements as well as in rougher country. Nocturnal, it sleeps during the day in caves and hollow logs, emerging at dusk to feed on insects, small lizards, birds, and rodents. The early colonists persecuted the native-cat because of its savage raids on their poultry; they didn't think of its value in keeping hordes of mice and rats in check. Along with many marsupials, native-cats were severely attacked by some sort of epidemic disease early in this century and disappeared from a great part of their range, apparently never to make a full comeback.

Numbat | *Myrmecobius fasciatus*
Rusty numbat | *M. rufus*

Numbat is the aborigine name for these small marsupials otherwise known as banded anteaters. Slightly larger than rats, they weigh about one pound. They are among the most colorful of marsupials, the back russet with 6 or 7 transverse bars in white or cream, the rusty numbat being the redder of the two. The muzzle tapers sharply to a small mouth, where a slender, cylindrical tongue, 4 inches long, flicks out with amazing speed to capture termites, the numbat's primary food. Daytime creatures, numbats live in hollow logs—logs often hollowed out by the termites they feast on. They are found in southwestern Australia, the rusty form in the eastern part of the range. Both are endangered by foxes, dogs, and cats, and especially by land clearance, which destroys their habitat. Of the two, the rusty numbat is the rarest.

Little planigale | *Planigale subtilissima*
Southern planigale | *P. tenuirostris*

Small, mouselike creatures, often referred to as flat-skulled marsupial mice, the planigales have remarkably flattened heads, which apparently evolved as a result of their lizardlike habit of sliding into ground crevices or through coarse tussocks of grass. The aptly named little planigale is probably the smallest existing marsupial, measuring only 1¾ inches, with a 2-inch tail. It is found in the Kimberly district in Western Australia. The southern planigale also has a 2-inch tail, but it measures a more robust 2¾ inches. It is also known as the dusky planigale because of its brown speckled coat.

Leadbeater's possum | *Gymnobelideus leadbeateri*

In many respects this little, 7-inch possum with grayish or brownish fur superficially resembles Australia's well-known sugar glider, but it lacks the gliding membrane. It lives in the thick forests of Victoria and was rediscovered in 1961 after being considered extinct for years. Its decline may have started

Eastern native-cat

Numbat

long ago in a period of ecological change, for it was already rare at the time that it was discovered in 1867.

Mountain pygmy possum | *Burramys parvus*
This small marsupial, with dense gray brown fur, prehensile fingers and toes, and a long, thin, scaly tail without prehensile undertip, was first described from subfossil remains found in caves in New South Wales and Victoria. The first living example did not show up until 1966, when a specimen was caught in a ski hut on Mount Hotham in Victoria. The generic name *Burramys* comes from the aborigine phrase *burra burra*, "place of many stones." Although it is certainly rare, the mountain pygmy possum may still survive in remote country.

Scaly-tailed possum | *Wyulda squamicaudata*
A completely scaly tail gives this possum its name and distinguishes it from other members of the family. It lives in Western Australia in mountainous country and is known to the older aborigines in one area as *illungalya* and to those in another as *ilangurra*. According to the aborigines, the animal normally is very rare, but at unpredictable intervals experiences a population boom.

Quokka | *Setonix brachyurus*
One of the small scrub wallabies, the quokka also goes under the name short-tailed pademelon. It is about as big as a hare, with a tail barely twice as long as its head. It also has a shorter foot than other wallabies and very short ears. The coastal thickets and swamps of Western Australia, especially in the southwest, constitute its habitat. It makes mazes of runways through coarse grass and thick undergrowth and has at times been mistaken for a large rat. Its popular name comes from the aborigines, who destroyed great numbers

Australian News and Information Bureau

Mountain pygmy possum

172

of quokkas by setting fire to the brush and spearing the animals as they fled the flames.

Stick-nest rat | *Leporillus conditor*

These little rats of southeastern Australia were known to the early colonists as "native rabbits" or "rabbit rats" because of their long ears. A blunt nose and generally fluffy appearance also helped to make them look like small rabbits with ratlike tails. They are now called stick-nest rats because of the ingenious nests they construct as protection from flesh-eating marsupials, dingos, foxes, owls, and other predators. The nests, usually based on a low-lying bush, are about 3 feet high and 4 feet in diameter, strongly woven of sticks. In areas where supporting bushes are not available, nests have been found with small stones on top to weight them down. Although plentiful on the plains of the Murray and Lower Darling rivers many years ago, the

Brush-tailed rat kangaroo
Vogt and Specht, *The Mammalia*

Quokka

173

stick-nest rats were becoming rare in the 1860s, as a result of hunting by the aborigines and increasing colonial activity, and they probably survive today only on the vast, inhospitable Nullarbor Plain.

False water rat | *Xeromys myoides*
This rat, about 4½ inches long with a 3-inch tail, earns its name because it is an aquatic feeder but lacks the elongated head, partially webbed feet, and stout white-tipped tail of the true water rats. Its color is slate gray above white underparts, and the feet and tail are covered with fine white hairs. It is a rare swamp dweller in Queensland.

Lydekker, *The Royal Natural History*

Thylacine

Lesueur's rat kangaroo

Brush-tailed rat kangaroo | *Bettongia penicillata*
Gaimard's rat kangaroo | *B. gaimardi*
Lesueur's rat kangaroo | *B. lesueur*
Plain rat kangaroo | *Caloprymnus campestris*
Queensland rat kangaroo | *Bettongia tropica*
The smallest members of the kangaroo family, these animals used to be known by the misleading term "kangaroo rat." Reversing the words is more appropriate and accurate, for they are not rodents but kangaroos with a ratlike appearance. Years ago they ranged through most of the continent outside the tropical regions of the north. Similar in habits, they are nocturnal creatures, lying during the daylight hours in grassy nests covered with debris or sometimes in small burrows. They use their slender tails not only to arrange the nesting material but to carry it, looping the tail around a tidy bundle of grasses as if it were a rope. In the early days they had no fear of people and often gathered around campfires at

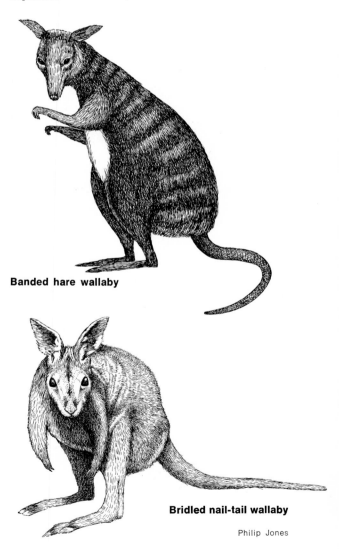

Banded hare wallaby

Bridled nail-tail wallaby

Philip Jones

174

night, darting in to snatch a morsel of food. They were so numerous that settlers regarded them as major pests raiding their crops and haystacks. With the spread of the fox and widespread poisoning, however, they are now extremely rare. Two species are extinct, and those listed here will probably follow that road unless sanctuaries are set aside where they can be protected from predators.

Thylacine | *Thylacinuscynocephalus*
Sometimes called the Tasmanian wolf or Tasmanian tiger, the thylacine is the largest of Australia's carnivorous marsupials. It is in no way related to the wolf, but is very much like that animal in appearance and predatory habits, providing a remarkable example of how animals evolve along parallel courses to fill certain ecological niches. The thylacine has a rigid tail like a kangaroo, and the female carries her young in a pouch forward of the hind legs. Normally the animal runs on all fours, but it has been seen bounding along, kangaroo fashion, on its powerful hind legs. It was once widespread over Australia, and fossil remains have been found in New Guinea. In the historic past it has been limited to Tasmania, where it became the sworn enemy of sheep ranchers, who hunted and poisoned it mercilessly. This pressure, plus an outbreak of disease—probably distemper—in 1910, dealt the thylacine such a blow that it never was able to recover. Occasional sightings and footprints in the mountainous west of Tasmania prove that at least a few survive, and the government, which once offered a bounty for each animal killed, now protects them and has established a reserve for them in the area where they have taken their last stand.

Banded hare wallaby | *Lagostrophus fasciatus*
Western hare wallaby | *Lagorchestes hirsu*
Hare wallabies were named for their harelike speed and jumping ability and their solitary habits. They are the smallest of the wallaby-kangaroo family. The banded hare wallaby, one of the most beautiful, is distinguished by the raccoonlike markings on its fur. It was once

plentiful in Western Australia but is now found in only a few isolated localities. The western hare wallaby is named *hirsutus* for the long reddish hairs on its lower back that give it a shaggy appearance; it won the nickname "whistler" from the early colonists because of its unusual habit of making a distinct whistling sound when pursued. Also from Western Australia, it has retreated into the interior desert country. A subspecies lives on several islands in Sharks Bay.

Bridled nail-tail wallaby | *Onychogalea fraenata*
Crescent nail-tail wallaby | *O. lunata*
A curious horny projection on the end of the tail accounts for part of the name of these small, silken-haired wallabies. In addition, the bridled form is so named because of the white markings on its head and shoulders, which suggest a bridle. The crescent form is similar, but the white shoulder stripe is limited to a moon-shaped mark. About 3 feet tall and delicately built, these wallabies carry their arms at an awkward angle to the body and rotate them when hopping, a practice that very quickly suggested the nickname "organ grinder" to the early settlers. Once plentiful across much of southern Australia, they are now absent or extremely rare over the entire range. Their flesh was considered excellent by the aborigines, who hunted them assiduously. But they did not go into decline until the white colonists came, bringing with them not only guns for hunting, but domestic animals and rabbits to compete with the wallabies for food, and the fox to prey on their young.

Australian News and Information Bureau by H. Brusse

Parma wallaby

175

Parma wallaby | *Macropus parma*
Also known as the white-throated wallaby, this distinctive small kangaroo was once abundant in sections of New South Wales but disappeared soon after Sydney was settled. In time, it came to be considered extinct. But in 1966 it was rediscovered on Kawau Island, thirty miles north of Auckland, New Zealand, where it had been introduced almost a century before by Sir George Grey, then the owner of the island. On Kawau, the wallaby was considered a pest, and thousands have been killed. With identification as a long-lost species, however, conservationists are fighting to save the white-throat and hope to reintroduce it to Australia.

Yellow-footed rock wallaby | *Petrogale xanthopus*
The little rock wallabies haunt the same rocky terrain favored by their giant wallaroo cousins, where they perform daring leaps from one outcrop to another. Chased from the rocks, they can climb leaning trees at top speed, much like tree kangaroos. They eat grasses, roots, bark, and tree foliage and can go for long periods without water. Despite their agility, they seem to have a low sense of self-preservation unless thoroughly alarmed, and fall comparatively easy prey to wild dogs, foxes, and large snakes. The yellow-footed species, also known as the ring-tailed rock wallaby, is distinguished not only by its brightly colored feet but also by its yellow ear-backs and the rings marking its tail. It was formerly fairly plentiful in South Australia, but is now making a last stand on the border of New South Wales. It is protected in South Australia, but its beautiful pelt still enters the fur trade.

Barnard's wombat | *Lasiorhinus barnardi*
Queensland hairy-nosed wombat |
L. gillespiei
The bearlike wombats, stockily built marsupials with broad heads, vestigial tails, and generally brownish fur, grow to about 4 feet in length and weigh about 70 pounds. They excavate extensive burrows, quite unlike their nearest living relatives, the tree-dwelling koalas. Nocturnal, they eat grasses, roots, and other vegetable matter, including crops, which makes them enemies of humans. The hairy-nosed wombats, which include these two forms, are so-named because hair grows in the area between the large nostrils; in the naked-nosed wombats the area, obviously, is hairless. The hairy-nosed wombats are also distinguished by their silkier fur, longer, more pointed ears, and smaller average size, about 3 feet. Both Barnard's wombat, the northern race, and the Queensland wombat have shrunk drastically in numbers and range since the spread of human settlements. Besides their raids on vegetable gardens and crops, they are branded as nuisances because their burrows are dangerous to horsemen and domestic cattle and make it difficult to eradicate rabbits by offering the elusive rodents too many places to hide.

Queensland hairy-nosed wombat
Lydekker, *The Royal Natural History*

Endangered Birds

Western bristlebird | *Dasyornis brachypterus longirostris*
Believed to be extinct after a brushfire apparently destroyed the last colony in the southwest of Western Australia in 1914, this 6-inch warbler was rediscovered in 1945 at Two People Bay. It disappeared again, but was subsequently seen in 1961, 1962, and 1963 in the area between Two People Bay and Taylor Inlet. Fortunately, this is the site of a sanctuary for the noisy scrub bird, and the bristlebird will undoubtedly benefit by the protection provided.

Eyrean grass wren | *Amytornis goyderi*
An extremely rare little warbler, the grass wren has been seen only a few times this century north of Lake Eyre in South Australia. It seems to be under no pressure from people or predators, so it may be a relict bird on a natural decline. The upper parts of its dull brown plumage carry prominent white streaks, and its beak is thick and sparrowlike.

Kakapo | *Strigops habroptilus*
This strange New Zealand bird was called "owl parrot" by the first European colonists because of its soft plumage, owllike face, and nocturnal habits. It is about 2 feet long, greenish yellow with dark barring, and feeds on berries, leaves, and an occasional lizard in the hillside beech forests that are its habitat. The kakapo is practically flightless—it uses its rounded wings for balance in running along paths through the forest and grassland, but occasionally climbs a tree and glides for a distance. Formerly widespread, the kakapo started on its decline with the arrival of the first Polynesian settlers in about A.D. 950, and the process accelerated with the coming of white people. The few surviving kakapos live in remote refuges in South Island's fiordlands and on Steward Island.

Kokako | *Callaeas cinerea*
These birds, dark bluish gray with a black band from eye to nostrils, exist in two races, one on New Zealand's North Island and one on South Island. Both have prominent face wattles, all blue on the northern bird and orange on a blue base on the southern bird. The North Island kokako, although much reduced from its abundant population of the early 1800s, still survives in scattered areas in fair numbers. The South Island kokako, however, victimized by introduced stoats and other predators, was becoming rare before this century started and has been sighted only a few times in the last thirty years.

New Zealand laughing owl | *Sceloglaux albifacies*
Called *whekau* by the Maoris, this relict bird has managed to remain off the extinct list by

New Zealand laughing owl
Philip Jones

virtue of the fact that it was last seen—and its unmistakable night sounds heard—in remote highland areas of South Island a number of times between 1914 and 1939. Ornithologists, not ones to give up easily, hope it may still survive in its last refuge, which is now being more assiduously explored by parties of naturalists.

Grass parakeets | *Neophema* and *Psephotus*
Australia has long been noted for its colorful parrots and parakeets, and many species still survive in healthy numbers. Several, however, have become quite rare and are in danger of extinction. The beautiful parakeet *Psephotus pulcherrimus,* with a limited range in southeast Queensland and contiguous parts of New South Wales, where it nests in termite castles, was down to an estimated 150 birds a decade ago. The paradise parakeet, *P. chrysopterygius,* has two races, a hooded form in the Northern Territory and a golden-shouldered race in northern Queensland. Both are local and now extremely rare. The orange-bellied parakeet, *Neophema chrysogaster,* is rare in both its races: the Tasmanian bird has not been seen since 1956, and the continental form since the late 1920s. The turquoise parakeet, *N. pulchella,* was believed to have only a

Australian News and Information Bureau

Kakapo

scattered distribution from Sydney to eastern Victoria, but in recent years has been reported several times from Queensland and may be staging a comeback. The scarlet-chested, or splendid, parakeet, *N. splendida,* has been reported enough times in recent decades from Western and South Australia to suggest that, rare though it might be, it still survives.

Forbes' parakeet (Forbes' kakariki) | *Cyanoramphus auriceps forbesi*
Orange-fronted kakariki | *C. Malherbi*
Forbes' parakeet, a subspecies of the yellow-crowned parakeet, was originally found on New Zealand's outlying southern islands of Pitt, Mangare, and Little Mangare. Since the late 1930s about 100 birds, all that are left, have survived on tiny Little Mangare. The small and rare orange-fronted kakariki, also called the alpine kakariki because of its preference for wooded hillsides, is found on South Island from Nelson to Fiordland. It has been reported by reliable observers in the Nelson Lakes National Park in recent years.

Ground parrot | *Pezoporus wallicus*
This small Australian parrot, a bird of the coastal area between hills and sea with quail-like habits, formerly was widely distributed in southern Australia and Tasmania. The Tasmanian and eastern races, while showing the effects of shrinking habitat, are in better shape than the western population, which was believed to be extinct earlier in this century. Since the 1940s it has been seen several times, and is fully protected by law.

Night parrot | *Geopsittacus occidentalis*
Little is known about this nocturnal, ground-living parrot from the arid interior of Australia, and nothing more may be learned, since it is very likely extinct. It was reported in Western and South Australia earlier in the last century, but after 1884 it apparently disappeared. It was seen again in spinifex country in Western Australia intermittently between 1912 and 1935, but disappeared again, except for one unconfirmed report in 1960. Total protection was granted in 1937, perhaps too late.

178

Chatham Island pigeon | *Hemiphaga novaeseelandiae chathamensis*

Half a century ago this brightly colored bird was still common in New Zealand and the Chatham Islands, 370 miles to the east, despite trapping by the Maoris, shooting by Europeans, and predation by introduced cats and weasels, and despite the fact that one egg normally made up a clutch. But destruction of its specialized forest habitat, where this pigeon feasted on certain fruits and shoots, has apparently done what the hunters could not do, and now it is in danger of extinction.

Piopio | *Turnagra capensis*

Two races of this "native thrush," which is more likely one of the races of the flycatchers, inhabit New Zealand, both called *piopio* by the Maoris in imitation of their loud, clear call. The North Island race has a gray breast and a white throat; the South Island bird is brown above and streaked with white and brown below. They both were plentiful until the latter half of the nineteenth century, when forest clearance reduced their habitat and introduced predators, such as stoats and cats, began taking an even larger toll. Only a few reports have been recorded from both islands over the past three decades, and if the piopio survives it has a most precarious hold on life.

New Zealand shore plover | *Thinornis novaeseelandiae*

Once widespread if not abundant in New Zealand proper, the shore plover survives now only on one of the Chatham Islands, Rangatira, in an area of less than one square mile. Here the birds are protected not only by law, but by the fact that cats and rats, very likely major agents in their extermination elsewhere, have not yet reached the tiny island.

Chatham Island robin | *Petroica traversi*

This small, dark-colored bird, also known as the black robin, is now limited to Little Mangare Island in the Chathams, an island so tiny it has only about one acre of vegetation on its rocky crown. Naturalists visiting the island late in 1973 found only 18 birds, and noted that each pair jealously defended its territorial rights. This intense competition for

Night parrot

Piopio

Rufous scrub bird

Stitchbird

Takahé

New Zealand bush wren

Philip Jones

179

limited living space shunted young, unpaired birds off to the fringe of the habitable area, where many died. To save the birds, a plan is being developed to capture and move them, pair by pair, across a 600-foot channel to a neighboring island with a larger tract of bushland. This will not be easy, since the naturalists will have to climb steep cliffs, and it would make more sense if the birds, which can fly, would discover the better habitat only 200 yards away themselves. But for some reason they don't or won't, so concerned New Zealand naturalists feel they must take on the responsibility.

Noisy scrub bird | *Atrichornis clamosus*
Rufous scrub bird | *A. rufescens*
Weak and reluctant fliers, Australia's primitive scrub birds are both relict populations, but the rufous form stands a better chance of survival in its range of forest reserves in New South Wales and Queensland. Its lighter colored relative to the west, the noisy scrub bird, was thought to be extinct after 1889. But it "came back from the dead" in 1961 when it was spied at Two People Bay in Western Australia, and later a small colony of 50 to 80 birds was found on the slopes of nearby Mount Gardner. A national park has been established in the area in an attempt to save these birds and other troubled wildlife of the region.

Stitchbird | *Notiomystis cincta*
One of New Zealand's three native honey eaters, the stitchbird once roamed all of North Island until European settlement began to disturb its habitat. Almost one hundred years ago it had withdrawn to such an extent that it survived only on 7,000-acre Little Barrier Island. The island was named a sanctuary in 1896, an act that certainly helped to save the stitchbird. An estimated 100 *hihi,* as they are called by the Maoris, exist there today. This is a 7-inch bird with a velvety black head, back, and throat, prominent white tufts on the side of the head, a band of yellow across the breast, and some yellow in the brown wings. Females are basically shades of brown, and show an olive tinge on the head.

New Zealand shore plover

Takahé | *Notornis mantelli*
A large, flightless bird that has become the symbol of the Ornithological Society of New Zealand, the takahé is one of the few living birds described from fossil material. These remains show that it was widely spread in fairly recent times, and it was assumed to have gone out of existence under pressure from Maori hunters and trappers, for the first European settlers found only 5 specimens. In 1948, however, it was dramatically rediscovered in a remote valley on South Island, and the valley was turned into a reserve almost immediately. Today the takahé is still in danger of extinction, with only 200 to 300 birds scattered in small groups over an area of 200 square miles. Attempts are being made, so far without success, to breed the bird in captivity.

Western whip bird | *Psophodes nigrogularis*
Once considered extinct, this shy and hard-to-find bird was rediscovered in 1939 in some strength near Gnowangerup, West Australia. It is at best now localized and extremely rare.

New Zealand bush wren | *Xenicus longipes*
The three races of this tiny forest foliage creeper are all rare and becoming rarer, surviving in small numbers in their respective ranges in North and South Islands and the outlying South Cape Islands. Ground feeders that are apparently losing their ability to fly, they undoubtedly have been persecuted by rats and other introduced predators. Another species, the Stephen Island wren, already flightless, became extinct in 1894 when the lighthouse keeper's cat hunted out and devoured the total remaining population of 20 or so birds.

Endangered Reptiles

Short-necked tortoise | *Pseudemydura umbrina*

Known also as the swamp tortoise, this is a rare species found only in three small swamps some twenty miles northeast of Perth, in Western Australia, although there is some reason to believe that its range once extended to other swamps in the area, since drained. It is now under government protection in a new 540-acre reserve.

Tuatara | *Sphenodon punctatus*

A living fossil, the tuatara is the last survivor of an order of reptiles that flourished some 200 million years ago, even before the peak period of dinosaurs, and may not have changed appreciably in 135 million years! Lizardlike in appearance, it varies in color from black brown to dull green, and sometimes shows a reddish tinge. Unlike most reptiles, it does not require high temperatures and is active even at 45 degrees Fahrenheit, doing most of its hunting at night. It has a very low metabolic rate, grows very slowly, and does not mate until the age of 20 or so. Its life span has been estimated at 100 to 300 years. The tuatara is also remarkable in that the male has no copulatory organ, mating being accomplished by cloacal apposition. Females store the sperm in their bodies and lay 5 to 15 soft-shelled fertilized eggs about 10 months later. The eggs take 13 to 15 months to hatch.

Once widely distributed over New Zealand, the tuataras are now limited to twenty small offshore islands, where they share ground burrows with petrels and shearwaters—usually, but not always, on an amicable basis. The Maoris have been blamed for their disappearance on the main islands, but some scientists believe ecological and climatic changes were a main contributing factor. Cats and rats constitute the tuatara's main enemies now that goats have been removed from most of the islands, and the ancient reptiles are fully protected. In fact, limits are set even on the number that scientific expeditions may remove for study.

Tuatara

THE ISLAND REALMS
Life in a Test Tube

Oceanic islands have been called the living laboratories of nature, for in long ages of isolation animals and plants followed their own evolutionary paths without interference from outside influences. It was in the Galapagos, for example—islands where flora and fauna of unexpected design flourished—that Darwin found living proof of his evolutionary theories.

As much as isolation, stability was an important ingredient in the development of life in the island realms. With no natural enemies, many island birds grew to gigantic size and lost their ability to fly: Madagascar's elephant bird, the moas and emus of Australasia, the famous dodo of Mauritius and other Indian Ocean islands. Other animals adapted to fill otherwise empty niches in the environment: the aye aye performing the role of a woodpecker on Madagascar, moas grazing like cattle on the grasslands of New Zealand, where no native mammals existed, the thylacine developing into a wolflike predator of Australia's other marsupials.

Island habitats that have reached a point of ecological balance over their lengthy periods of isolation have also been likened to Gardens of Eden. But paradise was inevitably lost with the arrival of human beings—particularly Westerners—and the other predators and domestic animals they brought with them. Successful creatures that for ages had lived unthreatened, unchallenged lives had little chance to adapt when the test tube of their environment was abruptly shattered. Many of them went swiftly into oblivion, and others even now are following in their wake.

Galapagos penguin

Preceding pages:
Cuban crocodile
Gladys Porter Zoo

Hawaiian dark-rumped petrel
Philip Jones

The Cahow: Future Uncertain

A large petrel, brown above and white below with a distinguishing white forehead, the cahow bred in great numbers on Bermuda until discovery of the island in the sixteenth century. Introduced pigs reduced the population, but in 1609, when the first English colonists arrived, the birds were still plentiful. With the famine of 1614–15, however, the starving settlers almost wiped out the birds, and the survivors were falling prey to the black rat, which had arrived with the ships.

Protective proclamations were issued in 1616 and 1622, but apparently too late—for 300 years nothing more was heard of the cahow, and it was presumed to be extinct. Ornithologists brushed off as cases of mistaken identity the claims of fishermen that they had sighted the cahow at sea, but in 1916 a bird found ten years earlier was positively identified as a cahow. More specimens began to show up, and finally, in 1951, an expedition located 7 nests on rocky, rat-free, offshore islets.

The cahow was still in trouble, however. Lacking soil in its new habitat to dig a nest burrow, it had taken to nesting in crevices in the cliffs. But its timing was wrong for that environmental niche, for just after its chicks hatched, the cliff-nesting tropic birds returned to breed in the same crevices, and almost all the cahow chicks were killed.

To help the cahow, game wardens in the newly formed conservation program designed baffles to put over each nest site—an artificial entrance with an opening big enough for a cahow but too small for a tropic bird. The hatching success of the cahow improved considerably, and the number of known breeding pairs rose to about two dozen. But then, just when daylight was showing, the rate of success dropped off drastically. Evidence seemed to point, as in other cases, to damage caused by pesticide residues.

The British government has set aside sanctuaries suitable for the cahow, predators are being removed, and artificial burrows are being constructed on the rocky offshore isles to separate the petrels and the tropic birds into their proper breeding niches once more. But until the pesticide problem can be resolved, the future of the cahow, and of many other sea birds, will remain in doubt.

Philip Jones

HAWAII

Endangered Mammals

Hawaiian hoary bat | *Lasiurus cinereus semotus*
Known in two color phases, red and gray, this small bat ranges primarily on Kauai, Oahu, Maui, and Hawaii. Removal of sheltering trees in many areas has brought about an apparent decline, and the present population is estimated at only a few thousand. Since this hoary bat is a nonsocial species, however, the fact that its population is scattered may make it appear less numerous than it actually is. The State of Hawaii has classified it as endangered and is considering banning the collection of specimens even for scientific studies.

Endangered Birds

Hawaiian coot | *Fulica americana alai*
Called *alae keokeo* by the Hawaiians, this bird differs from the American coot by having much darker gray plumage, a more slender white bill, and a much larger, whiter area on the forehead. A ducklike bird, it was on the game bird list until 1939, but there have been no open seasons since then. In addition to illegal hunting, its numbers are being depleted by destruction of wetlands and predation by dogs, cats, and mongooses. In 1972, only 352 birds were counted, a severe drop since the 1969 statewide census. Several key areas have been acquired for the establishment of refuges, and measures are being proposed to control predators that prey on this coot.

Hawaiian crow | *Corvus tropicus*
A black bird, tinged with brown on the wings, and with a more massive bill and higher-pitched voice than its mainland counterpart, this crow has never been found anywhere but along the western side of the island of Hawaii, in forested areas and mountains up to about 8,000 feet. It was numerous until the end of the nineteenth century, when farmers moved into the area, ripped out the forests, and began raising crops and running livestock. The crow was considered a natural enemy and was treated like vermin. Avian diseases from introduced species may also have taken a toll, and by 1937 a bird survey in the Kau and Puuwaawa forests turned up only a few specimens. Estimates of the population today range between 50 and 250. The crow is protected by state and federal law, but its range is outside the national park in southeastern Hawaii; sanctuaries have been proposed but are not yet fully implemented.

San Diego Zoo

Hawaiian duck

Hawaiian duck (koloa) | *Anas wyvilliana*
Formerly a resident of all the main islands of Hawaii except Lanai and Kahoolawe, the small brown-and-buff-streaked *koloa* is now restricted to Kauai, Hawaii, and to a smaller extent Oahu, where it has been reintroduced experimentally. Its reduction from its former numbers has been attributed to a change in agriculture in the islands, where areas devoted to the cultivation of rice and taro have been curtailed, and to the draining of other wetlands. Indiscriminate shooting by hunters, and nest ravaging by rats, cats, dogs, hogs, and mongooses have also contributed. Introduction of the mongoose on Kauai was prevented, which explains why the bird still survives there but has been lost on other islands. The

186

Laysan duck
San Diego Zoo

Hawaiian crow

Hawaiian gallinule

Hawaiian hawk

Kauai oo

Philip Jones

population has fluctuated in recent years, dropping to only about 200 in 1962, but seems to be on the rise now. State officials are conducting a propagation program with funds from the World Wildlife Fund, and there are hundreds of birds in captivity in aviaries in the United States and Europe available for stocking purposes. A key area at Hanalei has been acquired as a national wildlife refuge, and other sites are being sought.

Laysan duck | *Anas laysanensis*
In 1909, the year that President Theodore Roosevelt issued his famous bird-preservation order, a party of Japanese feather hunters landed on Laysan, at the far western end of the Hawaiian archipelago, and almost exterminated the small dark brown Laysan duck. Two years later conservation inspectors could find no more than 6 ducks on the island, their only home. The ducks made a comeback from that low point, but other disasters were to befall them—the introduction of rabbits resulted in virtually total destruction of the island's vegetation by 1923, and the duck population dropped to 7. Removal of the rabbits in 1926 brought another duck comeback, but in 1963, when the population was approaching 700, a violent hurricane swept hundreds of the weak-flying birds far out to sea, and many of them never made it back. The population is still fluctuating—down to 175 in 1972—and all the reasons are not known. Laysan Island is now a national wildlife refuge, and entry is restricted. More than 150 birds are in aviaries and zoos, and a captive breeding program has been designed to establish stocks of the duck on other islands.

Hawaiian gallinule (*alae ula*) | *Gallinula chloropus sandvicensis*
In Polynesian legend, the *alae ula* flew to the home of the gods, stole a burning brand, and brought fire to the early Hawaiian people. During the flight, the bird was scorched by the flames, a fact recorded in the name *alae,* which means "burned forehead." Ornithologists believe gallinules arrived in Hawaii long ago in the arms of storm winds and spread to wetlands on all the main islands except Lanai and Niihau. The Hawaiian gallinule is a darker

188

gray than the other common gallinules, with a brown back, white side stripes, greenish yellow legs tipped with red, and a red bill tipped with yellow. With the steady draining of freshwater ponds and other wetlands, its habitat has diminished. The bird survives, in numbers reduced to the hundreds, only on Kauai—where it is most numerous—and on Molokai, and Oahu.

Hawaiian hawk (io) | *Buteo solitarius*
The *io,* named for its high-pitched cry, is Hawaii's only native hawk and apparently has always been confined to the island of Hawaii. It has two color phases, light and dark. It has been victimized by hunters, both sportsmen and farmers, even though it is valuable as a controller of rats and mice. Although widely distributed on the island, its population has dropped into the low hundreds as its forest habitat has been reduced.

Nihoa millerbird | *Acrocephalus kingi*
Named after its dietary preference for large miller moths, this small, plain, brown and white reed warbler is confined to the wildlife refuge on Nihoa Island. For reasons that are still unknown, its population fluctuates between 300 and 600. It is not thought to be declining, but is considered vulnerable because of its extremely limited range of 174 acres, with its actual habitat only a part of the whole.

Kauai oo (oo aa) | *Moho braccatus*
The *oo aa* (pronounced "oh-oh-ah-ah")—dark gray, with a slender black bill, white streaks on its throat, yellow thighs, a white wing patch, and a pointed tail—is the last of Hawaii's five honey eaters, and it is on the verge of extinction. Its survival so far is probably due to the fact that Kauai has felt the impact of humans somewhat less than the other main islands, but the bird's condition is now precarious. A dozen *oo aa* were found in Alakai Swamp in 1960, 2 were seen nesting in a dead tree near Mount Waialeale in 1971, and 6 more were spotted in the same general area the following year. Hawaii has established a 10,000-acre refuge in the swamp, which may keep this and other troubled creatures alive.

Hawaiian dark-rumped petrel | *Pterodroma phaeopygia sandwichensis*
This large petrel, called *uau* in Hawaiian, has a white face, is dark on top and white below, and has white underwings. It formerly nested at high elevations on all the main islands, but is now limited to Haleakala crater on Maui and the flanks of Mauna Kea and Mauna Loa on Hawaii. At Haleakala National Park, where there are about 800 of the birds, evidence has shown that black rats ravage the chick population. There is no estimate of numbers on Hawaii, but the total is apparently quite low. Avian malaria, carried by mosquitoes, and predation by mongooses are believed to have reduced populations nesting at lower elevations. In addition to overall protection, the state is attempting to control predators on Maui.

Hawaiian stilt (aeo) | *Himantopus himantopus knudseni*
A black and white shorebird with very long red legs, the stilt was once native to all Hawaii's main islands but lost much of its habitat due to the draining and filling of marshes and shallow ponds. In days when it was more abundant it was classified as a game bird, but was removed from the list in 1941. Its population is down to little more than 1,000, with the largest numbers on Oahu and Maui. Refuges are being established.

Large Kauai thrush (Kauai omao) | *Phaeornis obscurus myadestina*
Small Kauai thrush (puaiohi) | *P. palmeri*
Molokai thrush (olomau) | *P. o. rutha*
These three birds are the last of Hawaii's thrushes; two other races already have gone into extinction. In fact, the Molokai thrush,

Small Kauai thrush
Philip Jones

The Hawaiian Goose: Saved

The arrival of white settlers in Hawaii started the downfall of the Hawaiian goose, or nene (pronounced "nay-nay"), and the gold rush in California almost wrote the final chapter. There is little doubt that the Polynesians hunted these heavily barred gray brown geese in their habitats on the volcanic slopes of the islands of Hawaii and Maui, but with nothing like the savagery of the civilized Westerner. Ship's crews, traders, and settlers took thousands of birds, and thousands more were salted down and shipped by clipper to California in a thriving trade that took the gold of the forty-niners in exchange for meat. Hunting was finally banned in 1911, but by that time there were precious few nene left to enjoy the peace.

The mission of preventing the nene's slide into extinction was taken on by a Hawaiian landowner, Harold C. Shipman. Starting in 1918 with a pair obtained from a friend, he bred a flock of 43 geese over the next thirty years; some he gave to a game farm on Oahu, some escaped back into the wild, and some died in the 1946 tidal wave that struck the islands. In the meantime, in 1927, the Hawaiian Board of Agriculture and Forestry had started a similar program and raised a flock of 42 birds. For some reason this effort was abandoned in 1935, and the flock was distributed to private aviculturists. Most of the birds were lost eventually in attempts to introduce the nene to other islands, and by 1947 only an estimated 50 geese, both wild and captive, survived in Hawaii.

Moving at last, the Hawaiian Board of Agriculture started another farm with a pair of females from Shipman's flock and two ganders, one from the Honolulu Zoo and the other one of the rare wild birds, caught in 1949. And in 1950, John Yealland, curator of the Severn Wildfowl Trust in England, visited Hawaii and brought home with him two of Shipman's precious geese for study and breeding. It was an embarrassing moment when both birds laid eggs, and Hawaiian officials hurriedly packed a bona fide gander on the next plane leaving for Europe.

The gander's name was Kamehameha, and he performed his duties in regal fashion. Nine goslings were born the first year in England, and by the time Kamehameha died in 1963 he had sired more than 230 birds—most of them in captivity in Europe and the United States but 50 flown back to Hawaii to restock Maui. The flock at the Hawaiian Board of Agriculture's farm in Pohakuloa also was building up, and the nene was reestablished in its old haunts on the slopes of Mauna Kea, Mauna Loa, Hualali, and Haleakala, where an estimated 1,000 birds had been released into the wild by 1972. Today, happily, the official state bird of Hawaii seems to be on its way to a full recovery.

Gladys Porter Zoo

brown on top and gray underneath, was thought to have disappeared between 1907 and 1936, but a pair was discovered at Puu Haha in 1963. Its range is limited to the native wet forests of eastern Molokai. The large Kauai thrush, a plump brown and gray bird with dark legs, was the most common forest bird on Kauai in 1891, but is now found in extremely reduced numbers only in the Alakai Swamp. The small Kauai thrush, distinguished by a white mark over its eye and flesh-colored legs, was probably always rare, certainly in more recent times. It, too, is recorded now only in Alakai Swamp. The primary reason for the decline of these fine songsters is the destruction of Hawaii's native forests, but diseases from introduced birds and predation undoubtedly have contributed; in Molokai, at least, rats have been seen in the trees. Establishment of Alakai Swamp Wilderness Preserve may help the Kauai birds, but proposals to construct a power and irrigation dam, with reservoir, on the edge of the swamp is certainly not in their interest.

The Honeycreepers of Hawaii

In the days when only the Hawaiians hunted them to make the spectacular royal feather robes with which they bedecked their chiefs, there were twenty-two full species of little honeycreepers on the islands. Today, eight are extinct, eight are considered in imminent danger of extinction, and the others are at least threatened with the same fate. Some are nectar feeders, with long bills; others have evolved sharp sickle bills for eating insects, parrot-type bills for eating seeds, and one, the rare akiapolauu, has developed a woodpecker-type bill. As with so many native birds, trouble came to the honeycreepers in the latter half of the nineteenth century when humans began to rip out the forests to make way for agriculture, introduce exotic birds (and their diseases), bring mongooses to the islands, and let dogs, cats, and hogs run wild. Sadly, twelve of the species were not discovered until 1893, when time had already begun to run out. Honeycreepers on the endangered list include the following:

Hawaii akepa | *Loxops coccinea coccinea*
An insect eater with a short, pale bill, orange red plumage on the male, green and yellow on the female, this bird once ranged all native forests, but now is confined to limited areas on Hawaii, on the slopes of Mauna Kea, Mauna Loa, and Hualalai. A dozen were seen in the Kau District in 1971, but only 4 since then.

Maui akepa (akepuie) | *Loxops coccinea ochracea*
Similar to the Hawaii akepa, with a sharp, blue

Dr. E. R. Degginger, APSA

Kagu

gray bill, the male *akepuie* varies from brownish orange to dull yellow, the females being dull yellow and olive green. Possibly extinct, the *akepuie* was last seen in 1950 on the south slope of Haleakala volcano, the only record since 1894.

Kauai akialoa | *Hemignathus procerus*
Brightly colored in greenish yellow, with a sickle bill more than 2 inches long—a third of its total length—adapted to probing for insects, this bird exists now in unknown numbers only in the Alakai Swamp of Kauai. Rare by 1920, it was seen in 1941 and 1957 in Kauai's upper rain forest, and in the swamp in 1960 and 1965. All these sightings were of individual birds.

Akiapolaau | *Hemignathus wilsoni*
Hawaii's "woodpecker," this small olive and yellow bird has a highly specialized bill—the lower mandible short and straight, the upper long and down-curved. It began retreating up the slopes of Mauna Kea and Mauna Loa on the island of Hawaii as the lowland forests were cut down. It was still fairly plentiful in 1950, but in more recent years has been seen only in small numbers.

Molokai creeper (kakawahie) | *Loxops maculata flammea*
Males are scarlet with brownish wings and tail; females are brown gray and white touched

191

Hawaii akepa

Kauai akialoa

Akiapolaau

Laysan finch

Mauai nukupuu

Crested honeycreeper

Philip Jones

with pink below. Forest clearance reduced this bird's habitat on the eastern side of the island of Molokai, and it was thought to be extinct until sightings in 1961, 1962, and 1963.

Oahu creeper (alauwahio) | *Loxops maculata maculata*
Males and females are both olive green above, yellow below, but the latter is duller. Both retain wing bars, present only in the juveniles of other species of creepers, and have slender, pointed bills. Only a few are left in Oahu's dwindling forests.

Laysan finch | *Psittirostra cantans cantans*
A finchlike honeycreeper, the Laysan finch is

thick billed, up to 7 inches long, brown with yellow head and breast. In 1923, when rabbits had almost denuded Laysan of vegetation, this bird was in serious trouble. But with removal of the rabbits it recovered, and there are now about 10,000 on Laysan and more than 400 more that have been transplanted to Southeast Island. It is on the danger list nonetheless because its confinement to two small islands renders it vulnerable to extinction.

Nihoa finch | *Psittirostra cantans ultima*
Similar to the Laysan finch in its brown and yellow coloring, but darker and smaller, the Nihoa finch has not declined appreciably, but is considered vulnerable because of its one-

island habitat. Its population fluctuates for unknown reasons and totaled 3,500 by estimate in 1972. In that same year, 10 birds still survived of the 36 transplanted in 1967 from Nihoa to Fern Island at French Frigate Shoals.

Crested honeycreeper (akohekohe) | *Palmeria dolei*
A beautiful 7-inch black bird with orange-tipped feathers, orange red at the back of its neck, and wearing a bushy white crest, it formerly ranged the mountain forests of both Molokai and Maui, but was last seen on the former in 1907. It is limited now to rain forests on the northeast slope of Haleakala on Maui.

Kauai nukupuu | *Hemignathus lucidus hanapepe*
A yellow and white bird with black feet and a long, sickle-shaped bill, the upper mandible twice the length of the lower, it is known to occur now only in Kauai's Alakai Swamp, where it was seen in the 1960s; the last previous sighting was in 1899, and it had been considered extinct.

Maui nukupuu | *Hemignathus lucidus affinis*
This bird is much like the Kauai race in coloration but with an olive back; females have a yellow stripe above the eye. Very uncommon, it was not seen after 1896 until 1967, when 2—and possibly 3—were reported from Kipahulu Valley.

Ou | *Psittirostra psittacea*
A 6-inch bird with a parrot-hooked bill, yellow head, and olive body, the ou formerly was widespread on the six major islands. Today, a small population survives on Kauai and possibly on Hawaii—one was seen in Hawaii Volcanoes National Park in 1970. On the other islands it is apparently extinct.

Palila | *Psittirostra bailleui*
A fruit eater with a thick, heavy bill, the palila has black wings and tail, yellow head and breast, white abdomen, and gray back. Its wide distribution on the mountainous slopes of the island of Hawaii has shrunk now to the mamane-naio forests at the 7,000–9,500-foot

level on Mauna Kea. In 1946 a colony on Mauna Loa disappeared, but 5 birds were recorded there again in 1964. The total population is estimated in the low hundreds.

Maui parrotbill | *Pseudonestor xanthophrys*
This small, olive green bird with yellow breast and yellow stripe over the eye uses its heavy parrot bill to get at beetle grubs in the bark and twigs of the koa tree. It is confined to Maui and lives in the rain forest on the northeast slope of Haleakala volcano between 4,000 and 6,000 feet. It is very rare, as the list of recent sightings shows—in 1950, on the north slope of the volcano, and in 1967 in Kipahulu Valley.

Ou

Palila

Maui parrotbill

Philip Jones

193

OTHER PACIFIC ISLANDS

Endangered Birds

Galapagos flightless cormorant |
Nannopterum harrisi
Although cormorants are known as strong
fliers and expert fishers, this brown bird with
a purplish gloss on its wings has lost the power
of flight, an evolutionary development
explainable by its residence in the Galapagos,
long isolated and free of predators. The bird is
as big as a goose, yet its wings are puny. It is
in trouble, of course, because the Galapagos
are no longer predator-free, and its population
is very low. These are quarrelsome birds in
captivity and bite savagely if bothered.

Palau ground dove | *Gallicolumba canifrons*
Palau fantail | *Rhipidura lepida*
Palau owl | *Otus podargina*
Sailors avoided the Palaus during much of the
nineteenth century because the natives were
known to be inhospitable—ferocious would be
a better word—and civilization therefore had
little influence there until after World War I.
Since then, many indigenous bird populations
have gone into decline, and these three are
particularly vulnerable because of their
limited distribution.

Tahiti flycatcher | *Pomarea nigra*
A blackish bird of the Society Islands, this
flycatcher was seen and described by J. R.
Forster, ship's naturalist on Captain Cook's
voyages in the late eighteenth century, but
rarely after that. It might have been presumed
extinct but for the great Whitney South Sea
Expedition of the American Museum of Natural
History, which found the bird thriving still in the
hill country of Tahiti. Its status today, however,
is unknown.

Galapagos hawk | *Buteo galapagoensis*
Described first in 1837 from material collected
by Charles Darwin, this sturdy bird was
common throughout the archipelago until well
into the twentieth century. Within the past forty
years or so, however, the bird has gone into
decline as human settlements expanded and
feral goats stripped the land of vegetation.
Chicken farmers took deadly aim at many
hawks, too, even though the birds seem to be
fairly catholic in their choice of food, preying
on iguanas, snakes, birds, and insects and even
eating carrion. Ecuador's 1959 law protecting
the Galapagos hawk and other creatures
indigenous to the islands may have come in
the nick of time, for a careful estimate in 1962
came up with a population count of no more
than 200 birds.

Kagu | *Rhynochetos jubatus*
Ornithologists have not decided whether this
strange, flightless, snail-eating forest bird of
New Caledonia should be classified with the
cranes and rails or with some other bird. It was
discovered after the French annexed the island
in 1853 and was even then withdrawing to the
mountains of the interior. Hunted by both the
Melanesian natives and the Europeans (the
latter for the plume trade), stripped of large
areas of its habitat by lumbering, mining,
burning, and the introduction of predators and
competitors, it has become extremely rare and
is fully protected. Hopes are that a kagu
reserve on the island will save this most
unusual 24-inch bird, which sports a
conspicuous crest of long gray plumes, a gray
body with wings banded in black and tipped
with white, orange eyes, reddish orange bill,
and long legs with reddish feet.

La Pérouse's megapode

Philip Jones

194

Galapagos hawk

La Pérouse's megapode | *Megapodius lapérouse*

Two races of this bird, one in the Palau group of the West Carolines and the other farther to the northeast in the Marianas, are extinct on most of the islands in their former range, and each may have a total population of less than 100. About the size of a small hen, they are dark birds, mostly black and brown, with small gray crests, yellow legs and feet, orange eyes, and orange or yellow bills.

Tinian monarch | *Monarcha takatsukasae*

A member of the flycatcher family, the monarch is endemic to the small Pacific island of Tinian, one of the Marianas. Its plumage is bright and cheerful: red brown on the back, gray on the head, with large white bars on the wings and tail feathers. It eats insects, fluttering after them in typical flycatcher style, in its woodland habitat. Little field work has been done in Tinian in recent years, but the monarch was already rare in 1945, when the last estimate was made, numbering only 40 to 50 birds.

Galapagos penguin | *Spheniscus mendiculus*

Only 20 inches long, the Galapagos penguin is a rarity among those cold-loving flightless birds—the only wholly tropical species. Living at the northern tip of the cold Humboldt current, they find ample fish in the cool, deep waters around the islands and many excellent nesting caves in the volcanic rock formations of the shore. Their population is low but relatively stable at 2,500; unfortunately, however, the penguin's future is uncertain because of abuse to the environment of the Galapagos Islands by unthinking humans.

Ponape great white-eye | *Rukia sanfordi*
Truk great white-eye | *R. ruki*
Unlike its relatives, the Truk great white-eye lacks the usually green coloration; it is sepia all over, with a black bill and reddish orange legs. Like the other "great" white-eyes, however, it lacks the ring of white feathers around the eyes and is considerably larger than many of the normal races of the bird. The Truk white-eye was discovered in 1895 on the island of Truk in the Carolines and is so rare that it apparently has not been recorded since. The Ponape bird, found only on the island of Ponape, is also rare. It was not discovered until 1931, when Japanese and American ornithologists, working separately, came upon it at the same time. The birds were seen again in 1947 by another expedition. Very little is known of their habits.

Okinawa woodpecker | *Sapheopipo noguchii*
Resembling no other woodpecker in the world, this 10-inch bird has a red back, pink belly, brown breast, dark brown wings with three conspicuous white bands or spots, a brown tail, and a cap that is red in the male and brown in the female. It is found only in the forests and bamboo grooves of Okinawa—but not much anymore, since deforestation and war may have combined to eradicate it. There are no current estimates of its numbers—if, indeed, any of the birds still exist.

Endangered Reptiles

Galapagos land iguana | *Conolophus subcristatus*
Barrington land iguana | *C. pallidus*
There are just two species of land iguanas peculiar to the Galapagos, the Galapagos race, which spread through most of the islands, and the Barrington, limited to the island that gave it its name. As with the Galapagos tortoises, these iguanas fell victim to human hunters, who took their skins, to predatory cats, introduced by Western sailing vessels, and to farmers and wild goats, each of which, in his own way cleared away much of the protective vegetation. Galapagos land iguanas still

survive in varying numbers on Narborough, Albemarle, Indefatigable, Seymour, and South Plaza but are probably extinct on James Island. The Barrington land iguana population was estimated at 300 in the 1960s, with very few young in evidence. Based on the experience of tiny South Plaza Island, where iguana numbers rose satisfactorily after the goats were cleared out, experts believe the fate of both species rests on a program of goat removal. This is especially important on Barrington, where Galapagos hawks prey on the exposed iguana young, adding an extra hazard.

Galapagos giant tortoise | *Testudo elephantopus*
In Spanish, *galapago* means "turtle," and the group of islands 500 miles off the coast of Ecuador that carry the name once swarmed with these huge tortoises, up to 4 feet long and weighing 500 pounds. But in the 400 years after the Spanish discovered the islands, pirates,

New York Public Library

Galapagos giant tortoise

sealers, whalers, and merchant sailors slaughtered so many for their meat that by the latter half of the nineteenth century few were left. Cats and rats, introduced by the sailing ships ravaged nests and fed on the young, their task made easier by wild goats, who stripped many areas of covering vegetation. All Galapagos tortoises are now protected by law, and all uninhabited islands in the group, along with the western section of Indefatigable Island, have been declared reserves. Small wild populations still exist on these islands, and several hundred more are held in zoos around the world. A number of zoos have had success in breeding the Galapagos tortoise in captivity; the San Diego Zoo alone reported 32 hatchings since 1958.

THE CARIBBEAN

EndangeredMammals

Cuvier's hutia | *Plagiodontia aedium*
Dominican hutia | *P. hylaeum*
Of the four species that make up this genus, two are extinct, probably as a result of overhunting by early populations on the island of Hispaniola, jointly occupied by Haiti and the Dominican Republic. The remaining two are also in trouble because they are considered good to eat—by dogs, cats, and introduced mongooses as well as by people. Large terrestrial rodents, hutias resemble coypu. Cuvier's, named after the French naturalist who discovered it in 1836, is about 18 inches long, 6 inches of which is naked, scaly tail. Its dense fur is mixed with longer hairs, some black and some gray, tipped with dull yellow brown. Apparently limited to Haiti, it was thought to be extinct until 1947, when a specimen—only the second seen by modern man—was found in a remote area. The

Dominican hutia, with a larger body, shorter tail, longer claws, and darker fur, was discovered in 1923 in the Dominican Republic and was thought at first to be identical with its relative in Haiti. Little is known of the habits of these rare creatures, but they are believed to be nocturnal vegetarians. Unlike so many other rodents, their productive rate is thought to be low, a fact that, if true, would help to explain the animal's inability to cope with the pressures on them.

Cuban solenodon | *Atopogale cubana*
Haitian solenodon | *Solenodon paradoxus*
Solenodons are about the size of small cats, but with their long, slender snouts and long, naked tails they look more like rats or shrews. Equipped with sharp claws, they are nocturnal hunters for insects and small animals, but also eat roots and fruit. The two species, the only surviving members of a primitive family, occupy the neighboring islands of Cuba and Haiti and are distant relatives of the tenrecs of Madagascar. Slow and clumsy, they have become threatened by the introduction of mongooses, cats, and dogs to the islands, as well as by destruction of the indigenous forests and the raids of collectors seeking specimens for the world's zoos.

American Museum of Natural History

Cuvier's hutia

Cuban solenodon
Lydekker, *The Royal Natural History*

197

Endangered Birds

Grenada dove | *Leptotila wellsi*
A drab brown and wine-colored bird, about 12 inches long, the Grenada dove is so rare that it may be going into extinction before scientists can find out why. Its habits are little known; even its call is a mystery. Between 1920 and 1925 several were brought to London and bred in captivity, but since 1929 they have been considered virtually extinct on Grenada and nearby Glover's and Green islands. Specimens were seen in 1961 and 1963, however, and the possibility exists that a tiny population may survive in a remote area on Grenada.

Cuba hook-billed kite | *Chondrohierax wilsonii*
Grenada hook-billed kite | *C. uncinatus*
Called *caguarero* in Spanish, the Cuba hook-billed kite was so rare in the woods south of Guantanamo in 1950 that it was thought to be near extinction. Little more is known of it today. The Grenada kite, rare also in Grenada and Trinidad, may still occur in Central and South America.

Bahamas parrot | *Amazona leucocephala bahamensis*
One of the large, colorful, "talking" parrots of the West Indies, this race that formerly ranged through much of the Bahamas survives only in the remote northern part of Great Inagua, where it numbers probably less than 1,000 birds. Habitat destruction as the forests were cut down, together with hunting, undoubtedly led to its decline.

Imperial parrot | *Amazona imperialis*
Red-necked parrot | *A. arausiaca*
Dark green above and metallic purple below, with a black ruff about the neck, the large Imperial parrot is considered the most handsome of them all. It is limited to Dominica, where human intrusion and hunting have chased it into the high mountain forests, which it shares with the also threatened red-necked parrot. It was considered scarce in the 1920s and is classified as rare today. It is nominally protected by laws against hunting, but has no sanctuary in which to find safety.

Puerto Rican parrot | *Amazona vittata*
A foot long, bright green, with red forehead, blue primary wing feathers, and flesh-colored bill and feet, this parrot is now confined to the Luquillo Experimental Forest. Its decline was brought about by destruction of forests for agricultural use, and nest raiding by rats and predatory birds. No hunting is allowed in the Luquillo area, and rat control programs are being developed. But time may have run out—only 15 to 20 birds were left at last count.

St. Lucia parrot | *Amazona versicolor*
St. Vincent parrot | *A. guildingi*
Widespread in the 1940s, the handsome St. Lucia parrot went into swift decline during the following decade, appearing only in the mountain forests in the center of the island. Pigeon hunters must bear much of the blame, along with hunters of live birds, who trap for the pet trade. The St. Vincent parrot, resident on a much smaller and less-cultivated island, does not depend so much on forest areas for nesting and is therefore holding its own better than other parrots. There are probably several hundred still surviving, but illegal hunting makes their future insecure.

St. Vincent parrot

Black-capped petrel

White-breasted thrasher

Martinique brown trembler

Zapata wren

Philip Jones

Black-capped petrel | *Pterodroma hasitata*
Known by the Caribbean Indians as *diablotin,*
"little devil"—a name still in use today—this
dark brown bird with white on its neck, rump,
and tail formerly nested in hillside burrows
and cliff caves on Jamaica, Guadeloupe, Haiti,
Dominica, and Martinique. The spread of
humans, the rats and mongooses they brought
with them, and several great earthquakes all
contributed to the decline of the birds. Hunters
accompanied by dogs and equipped with long,
hooked poles attacked the birds in their
burrows during the breeding season. They
were especially intent upon taking the young,
called "cottons," which were considered
particularly succulent. Since the petrels lay
only one egg a year, this kind of senseless
predation could have only one result. Until
recently, the only record of *diablotins* consisted
of sightings at sea, a fact which suggested
that somewhere a breeding ground was still
in operation. This was found in 1963 on the
Morne la Salle in Haiti, where a surprisingly
large population of about 4,000 breeding birds
was counted. Now survival of the bird will
depend entirely upon protection of it by
the Haitian government.

Puerto Rican plain pigeon | *Columbia
inornata wetmorei*
Once thought to be extinct, this grayish brown
pigeon with a pink violet head has reappeared
in small numbers, occasionally in the markets
of Ponce; although hunting of it is prohibited,
some shooters do not distinguish between it
and other wild pigeons. It is apparently
limited to a woodland near Lago de Cidra, and
possibly in nearby lowland forests. If observers
who believe it is increasing in numbers are
correct, there may be several hundred birds
alive today.

White-breasted thrasher | *Ramphocinclus
brachyurus*
Eight-inch birds with long, thin bills, brown
with pure white breasts, these thrashers are
found only on Martinique and St. Lucia. They
resemble no other thrashers alive today.
Exceedingly rare, they were thought to be
extinct for many years. A small population of

199

the Martinique race was found in 1950 on the Caravelle isthmus, and a pair was seen there in 1966. The St. Lucia thrasher was reported in 1961, and more recently near Castries. Since these unprotected birds are terrestrial, introduced predator animals may be hastening their descent into oblivion.

Grand Cayman thrush | *Turdus ravidus*
Little is known about this handsome gray and white robin-sized bird with coral red bill, feet, and eye-ring, and it may be too late to find out more. Restricted to Grand Cayman Island, it was rare as long ago as 1911, and the last sighting was recorded in 1938. Woodland destruction may have contributed to its disappearance, but ornithologists are at a loss to explain why it failed to adapt to a changing environment, as do so many other thrushes.

Martinique brown trembler | *Cinclocerthia ruficauda gutturalis*
This is one of six 10-inch birds of the Lesser Antilles with long, thin bills and color varying from dark brown and gray to light, known for their strange habit of shivering or trembling. The Martinique trembler, known locally as the *grive trembleuse,* was extremely rare as far back as 1879, a result of heavy hunting by humans, rats, and mongooses. It was last sighted in 1964, but may still survive despite the complete absence of protection.

Semper's warbler | *Leucopeza semperi*
This 6-inch gray and white bird, large for a warbler, is peculiar to St. Lucia, where it may already be extinct. Very little is known about its habits except that it once was fairly common in mountain forests, where it nested in or near the ground in undergrowth. It has been sighted only three times in the last forty years—in 1934, 1947, and 1961.

Puerto Rican whippoorwill | *Caprimulgus noctitherus*
This dark, mottled nightjar with long bristles around its mouth has had an unusual history. It was first discovered in a cave excavation in 1919, in the form of fossil remains. Then a skin dating from 1889 came to light, proving

the bird was still alive. For years no further specimens were found, however, and it was assumed to have become extinct. But in 1961 the bird was rediscovered, and it is estimated today to have a population of about 300 pairs living in three forest areas. Reduction of Puerto Rico's woodlands, pollution by expanding industries, and predation by introduced mongooses pose the biggest threats to its continued existence.

St. Lucia house wren | *Troglodytes aedon mesoleucus*
St. Vincent house wren | *T. a. musicus*
Of several subspecies of house wrens in the West Indies, two are extinct (Martinique and Guadeloupe), three are abundant and in no danger (Tobago, Grenada, and Dominica), and two are now extremely rare (St. Lucia and St. Vincent). Why the wrens seem to have adapted to human settlement on some islands and not on others is a puzzle, but it is interesting to note that Dominica, where the bird is still widespread, has no mongoose population. In Grenada the bird has become a regular dweller in the suburbs, as is the habit of the wrens of the mainland.

Zapata wren | *Ferminia cerverai*
Zapata rail | *Cyanolimnas cerverai*
Both these birds are included in the *Red Data Book* as a precautionary measure, for they are limited to a few square miles of wilderness in and around Cuba's Zapata Swamp. They would be in dire trouble if the swamp were drained, as has been proposed.

Endangered Reptiles

Cuban crocodile | *Crocodylus rhombifer*
A small species barely reaching 7 feet in length but one of the most aggressive of all crocodiles, the Cuban species is marked by a raised, triangular lump in front of the eyes, similar to the Siamese animal. Mature specimens are dark, some almost black, with light yellow spots on the hind legs. Once ranging over much of Cuba's west-central

section and the Isle of Pines, this crocodile was hunted for its hide until only about 500 were left, most of them in the half-square-mile confines of Zapata Swamp. The swamp is now a refuge, and hunting of this rare animal is forbidden by the Cuban government.

Puerto Rican boa | *Epicrates inornatus*
A 6-foot-long gray or brown serpent, this boa probably once ranged throughout the larger islands in the Puerto Rican area. Today it numbers only about 200 in Puerto Rico itself, with others possible in the United States and British Virgin Islands. One specimen was found during destruction of a wall in St. Thomas, and there have been isolated reports from Tortola. Predation by mongooses is believed to be a major cause of the snake's decline. Automobile traffic accounts for some deaths, and the Puerto Rican people exhibit the usual human reaction to snakes, killing every one they come across.

INDIAN OCEAN ISLANDS

Endangered Mammals

Eastern woolly avahi | *Avahi laniger laniger*
Western woolly avahi | *A. l. occidentalis*
A few decades ago both of these races of the avahi were fairly common in Madagascar, but the uncontrolled burning and clearing of their forest environment has reduced their numbers and made their condition precarious. They are also taken by the local inhabitants for food, but this has always been so and the animals could handle this cropping if it were not for the loss of habitat. The eastern race formerly inhabited the entire forested region of northeastern, eastern, and south-central Madagascar; the western version was found on the northwestern coast as far south as the Bay of Bombétoka. The avahi is a small animal with a 1½-foot body

and a tail at least as long. The woolly fur is soft and thick, grayish brown with a yellowish tinge in the western race, reddish brown with black tips in the eastern. Both have large eyes and small ears, and are much more arboreal than other members of the Indrid family. They appear to be strictly vegetarian, feeding on leaves, buds, and bark, and occur only singly or in pairs. Nocturnal creatures, they spend the day sleeping in dense undergrowth, in the fork of a tree, or clinging to a branch.

Eastern woolly avahi
Philip Jones

201

Aye-aye
Lydekker, *The Royal Natural History*

Aye-aye | *Daubentonia madagascariensis*

The strange little aye-aye, named for the grating cry it occasionally utters, is the most primitive of all the primates. About the size of a cat, it looks like a type of squirrel and at one time was considered part of the rodent family. It has coarse black fur, large ears and eyes, a bushy tail, and large, curved, rodentlike incisors that continue to grow throughout its life. Most unusual of all are its feet and hands, especially the elongated middle finger on the latter. The aye-aye is an arboreal insect eater, and it uses its keen sense of hearing and smell to locate larvae and wood-boring insects under the bark of dead branches. Now the incisors come into play, quickly gnawing a hole in the wood—and then the long, thin finger, used to hook or skewer the prey. To supplement its diet the aye-aye also eats fruits, sugarcane, and bamboo pith.

These animals are nocturnal and live singly or in pairs. Females build intricate nests high up in the trees and like most lemurs bear one offspring. Aye-ayes have been objects of awe and superstition with many Malagasy people. Some believed the animals to be the reincarnation of their forefathers, and when they found a dead one they buried it with honor. Others believed that if they touched an aye-aye they would be dead within a year; considered an evil omen, therefore, the aye-aye was killed if it appeared in a native village— and if it escaped, the village was abandoned. The aye-aye no longer ranges through most of eastern Madagascar. Only about 50 of them survive in the wild in the remnants of the northeastern coastal forests, and when these woodlands go the aye-aye will probably go, too. In an effort to save the animal, the IUCN (International Union for Conservation of Nature and Natural Resources) in 1965 backed a move to set up a reserve on the island of Nossi Mangabé, off Madagascar. Four males and five females were released there with the hope that they will form a breeding colony.

Indri | *Indri indri*

This 3-foot-tall black and white animal with a very short tail, largest of the lemuroids, earned its name through a language mix-up. Spying the creature in the trees, native guides leading early naturalists through the forests of Madagascar would point and shout, *"Indri! Indri!"* In their language they were saying, "Look, look!" The naturalists, however, thought that was the name of the animal. Later, naturalists collected many fascinating native legends about the indri, which were held in superstitious awe by most of the early peoples. Some of the most interesting included the belief that the indri, like the aye-aye, were reincarnations of the dead, that plants used in the animal's nest would cure almost any illness, that parent indri trained their young to leap through the trees by tossing them back and forth in the air, that a spear thrown at an indri would be caught and thrown back with unerring accuracy, and that they could be trained to hunt like dogs. This last item may have a connection with the name "dog of the forest," applied to the indri because its loud howling can be heard for miles.

Indris are nocturnal animals, traveling in small groups and eating leaves, fruits, and other vegetable matter. In the trees they leap from one vertical branch to another, catching hold with their powerful hind feet. On the ground they walk upright or hop. They are sometimes seen basking in the sun with arms extended, giving rise to the legend that they worshiped the sun. Loss of habitat is hurting the indris as it is the other members of the family. Hunting does not seem to be much of a contributing factor in their decline, for in addition to the sacred awe the animal has enjoyed, its flesh is tough and stringy and not especially palatable even to those who enjoy the flavor of it.

Indri

Lydekker, *The Royal Natural History*

Madagascar's lemurs

With the devastation of Madagascar's forest lands and the outward expansion of its human population, all the lemurs, small relatives of monkeys found only there and on some smaller outlying islands, are in danger. There are two subfamilies in the Lemuridae—greater lemurs and dwarf, or mouse, lemurs—each of which has three genera and a number of species. Those discussed here are representative of the entire large group.

Broad-nosed gentle lemur | *Hapalemur simus*

The broad-nosed gentle lemur is also called the reed lemur for its habitat—it lives now only in reed beds around Lake Alaotra. Its upper coat is gray tinged with red, its underparts, limbs, and tail are gray, and its chest and chin are yellowish or dirty white. It grows to about 18 inches in length, with a tail equally long, and all its teeth except the molars have serrated edges for handling the bamboo shoots and other tough fibrous material that make up its diet. These lemurs are nocturnal and live alone or in small groups. For a time they were thought to be extinct, and certainly are not far from that unenviable status.

Fat-tailed lemur | *Cheirogaleus medius*

Fat-tailed lemurs are so called because in Madagascar's hot, dry season, when food is hard to find, they go into a comatose state known as estivation, similar to the hibernation of other animals in cold climates, during which they are nourished by the fat stored in their tails. About the size of a large rat, they are gray or brown on top, whitish below, and have large, dark-ringed eyes in a wide, catlike face. A nocturnal species, they survive now only in two locales, one in the northwest of the island and the other in the southwest.

Fork-marked mouse lemur | *Phaner furcifer*

The only member of its genus, the fork-marked mouse lemur can grow to an overall length of 11 inches. The adjective "mouse" is descriptive only of its appearance, since it has no relationship to rodents. The reason for the rest of its name is obvious: a dark stripe runs along its spine, forking at the crown of the head and

Lydekker, The Royal Natural History

Fork-marked mouse lemur

continuing down each side to form rings around the eyes. The bushy tail is longer than the body and darker than the brownish gray coat and is tipped with white or black. An agile nocturnal feeder, this little lemur lives in the trees, spending its days in hollows that it often shares with bees, perhaps, as it is popularly believed, to gorge itself on honey. It was abundant until the 1930s, but now seems to be limited to only a few areas.

Mongoose lemur | *Lemur mongoz*

The mongoose lemur was always considered uncommon, and is even rarer now. It occurs in a restricted area in the northwest of Madagascar and on two of the Comoro Islands. Both sexes are colored similarly, brownish gray above and white below, with one major exception—the cheeks of the male are red and those of the female are white. Smaller than a cat, the mongoose lemur is arboreal and diurnal, and travels in groups of three or four.

Verreaux's sifaka

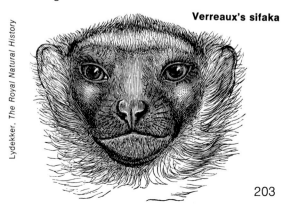

Lydekker, The Royal Natural History

203

Diademed sifaka | *Propithecus diadema*
Verreaux's sifaka | *P. verreauxi*

These two species of Madagascar's sifakas, including a number of races, were once widely distributed on the island, the diademed in the forest and scrub country along the eastern length, Verreaux's in the woodlands of the west. Probably the best leapers in the family, with tree-to-tree jumps of 30 and 40 feet, they are essentially arboreal but move about on the ground occasionally with awkward hops. They are diurnal and vegetarian, seldom fight except during mating season, and are much quieter than the other Indrids. Verreaux's sifaka, which includes five races (Verreaux's, Coquerel's, Van der Decken's, Forsyth Major's, and the crowned), ranges in color from almost all white to white with patches of maroon or black on the head, belly, back, or limbs. The diademed sifaka, with its three races (Milne-Edward's, silky, and black), is slightly larger and also basically white, but with patches of orange, deep brown, and black. The face and ears in both species are naked and black. Lengths run from 18 to 22 inches, with a tail about as long. The legs are long and strong, and the big toe is almost as large as the rest of the foot—a powerful tool for catching and holding an upright tree limb. A narrow, vestigial membrane stretching from arms to legs along the sifaka's sides is undoubtedly of great assistance in the spectacular leaps the animal makes.

Endangered Birds

Mauritius olivaceous bulbul | *Hypsipetes borbonicus olivaceous*

A thrushlike bird known locally as *merle,* this olive brown bulbul with orange bill and legs lives in swampy areas and woodlands above the 3,300-foot level of Mauritius, principally on the leeward side. It is now probably rarer than the similar subspecies on neighboring Reunion, where the bird population was drastically reduced by a cyclone in 1948 but was able to recover in the island's still-thick forests. The problem with the Mauritius bird comes from the fact that its habitat has been extremely reduced—only about 20 percent of the island's woodlands are left.

Philip Jones

Seychelles kestrel

Seychelles paradise flycatcher

Seychelles paradise flycatcher | *Terpsiphone corvina*

Also known as the Seychelles black flycatcher, this attractive little bird is marked, in the male, by central tail feathers that may reach a total length of 21 inches. Once known on several of the islands of the group, it is now restricted to the rather small island of La Digue. These birds are in danger not only because of their limited habitat, but also because of human thoughtlessness and predation. Customarily, paradise flycatchers build cuplike nests of grass and other plant materials, binding them with a network of threads from spider webs to a fork far out on a branch—so far out that the slender twigs will not support the weight of such predators as cats, rats, and snakes. Unfortunately, however, the birds tend to nest close to the edges of clearings, and on heavily populated La Digue there are many people who also use the clearings and who have no compunctions about knocking the nests down or stealing the eggs.

Seychelles fody | *Foudia sechellarum*

This is the only weaver bird of the Seychelles, but unlike its relatives on nearby islands, it is dull brown instead of red and has a trace of yellow on the face. It is now restricted to three small islands having a total area of only about 1,000 acres, and it may have a total population of only a few hundred. Habitat destruction has been its primary enemy: on Marianne Island, where it is now extinct, the original vegetation is all gone, supplanted now by rundown plantations where feral cats and dogs roam.

Mauritius kestrel | *Falco punctatus*

Kestrels are a distinctive group of falcons, worldwide in distribution, which seek ground prey rather than insects or other birds in flight. The Mauritius kestrel, one of the smallest, was once fairly common on the island but apparently is being pushed into extinction by gun-toting farmers who object to the bird's raids on their chicken yards—a reason given substance by the kestrel's local name, *mangeur de poules*.

Seychelles kestrel | *Falco araea*

Another small kestrel, only 8 to 9 inches long, this little falcon has experienced a drastic population crash since 1940, when it was common to most islands of the group. It is now limited to Mahé, and naturalists are at a loss to explain its decline. It feeds primarily on lizards, which are still plentiful, so that food supply is not a problem. Some sources say that the birds are so comparatively tame that they become easy marks for children armed with slingshots. Others point to the barn owl, introduced from South Africa to control rats, and believe that it is disturbing the falcon by taking over its nesting and roosting sites.

Seychelles magpie-robin | *Copyschus sechellarum*

In 1958 this thrush-sized songbird, once thought to be extinct, was reported to be increasing in numbers. Either the information was erroneous or a terrible catastrophe occurred, for in 1960 only 10 pairs of birds could be found on Frégate, a number that dropped to only 6 pairs a few years later, with even fewer on one or two of the other islands. Reasons given for the widespread destruction of this little gray blue bird with white wing coverts include thoughtless slingshot hunting by children—and even some adults—predation by introduced cats, rats, and cattle egrets, and competition for available food from introduced mynah birds.

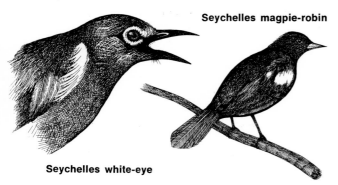

Seychelles magpie-robin

Seychelles white-eye

Philip Jones

Seychelles owl | *Otus insularis*

Most of our information about this little 10-inch owl, dark chestnut with mottled head, dappled neck, and black streaks down the feather shafts, comes from stuffed specimens in museums. In fact, it was considered extinct, for it had been last reported in 1906 and could not be found by several expeditions in the Seychelles between 1931 and 1936. In 1959, however, a tiny colony was discovered deep in the mountains of Mahé, and ornithologists assume the bird is still breeding there. Their other assumption—that the bare-legged scops owl, as it is sometimes called, has been replaced over its former wide range by competition from the introduced South African barn owl—suggests that it will indeed go into extinction before too long.

Mauritius ring-necked parakeet | *Psittacula krameri echo*

A 12-inch bird, the male of this rare parrot has a green head topped with blue, a green body, yellow tints on its wing coverts, bluish central tail feathers, a rose-colored collar, and a red bill. The female differs considerably, being all green with a black bill. Reports from Mauritius suggest that the birds survive in small numbers in the forests, saved from extinction by the fact that they are not frequent visitors to cultivated gardens.

Long-tailed ground roller | *Uratelornis chimaera*

A russet back and mottled tail provide excellent camouflage for the ground roller as it seeks insects in piles of dead leaves. The tail that gives the bird part of its name is up to 8 inches long, fully as long as the body. Bright blue feathers line the tail and wings, but they show best when the bird flies, which it does rarely, for true to the rest of its name, it spends most of its time on the ground. One of five species of ground rollers native to Madagascar, it occupies a narrow strip of dry, scrub brush country extending about 125 miles along the coast. The other species, occupants of the rain forest, face a precarious future as their habitat is opened to development. But the long-tailed ground roller is vulnerable now to the rapid expansion of human activities.

Small-billed false sunbird | *Neodrepanis hypoxantha*

Sunbirds are tiny, brilliantly colored birds with fine, long bills, often curving downward. They belong to the family of nectar feeders, the Old World counterpart of American hummingbirds. Little is known about Madagascar's small-billed false sunbird except that it is very similar to the true sunbird, with a slender build and a thin, down-curved bill. It has long been rare—only 9 specimens have been collected from the forests of central Madagascar, and with the rapid destruction of these forests in recent years the bird may well be extinct.

Rodriguez warbler | *Bebrornis rodericanus*
Seychelles warbler | *Nesillas sechellensis*

The Seychelles warbler, a sweet-singing bird first described in 1877, is dull olive green on the head and back and dull yellow beneath. Its local name is *petit merle*. It has been extinct for years on the larger islands where it once roamed and is now confined to the sixty-acre islet of Cousin. In all, about 45 birds live there in mangrove swamps, shoreline undergrowth, and coconut groves. The population may be stabilized, considering the limited size of the habitat, and since cats and rats have not yet been introduced the race may be safe for the moment. But the very smallness of the habitat makes the bird's condition precarious, for a single accident of nature, or the arrival of a predator, could wipe it out of existence. The related Rodriguez warbler, named for the island it inhabits, was down to a population of only 10 to 20 birds in 1964, and extinction seems imminent.

Seychelles white-eye | *Zosterops modestus*

There are about eighty-five species of white-eyes, most of them remarkably alike—green head, body, and tail, gray or yellow below, and sometimes with reddish brown on the flanks. Tiny birds with thin bills, they gain their common name from the ring of white feathers around the eyes. They are almost entirely arboreal, and as the trees of their widespread range through Africa, Asia, and Australasia are cut and burned, they will begin to disappear. This was the likely fate of the chestnut-flanked white-eye of the Seychelles *(Zosterops semiflava),* which is probably extinct. The only other white-eye in the islands, the grayish brown Seychelles white-eye, is confined to the small section of forest still standing in the hills of Mahé Island, and may soon follow its relative.

Endangered Reptiles

Madagascar radiated tortoise | *Testudo radiata*

Considered one of the world's most striking turtles, the radiated tortoise of Madagascar carries a black or dark brown high-domed shell marked with radiating gold lines. These lines have been likened to sunbursts, or at least to half-sunbursts, since the lines are stronger going downward. About 18 inches long, this tortoise can weigh more than 20 pounds, and thrives on a diet of cactus in its scrub desert environment. Like so many creatures in Madagascar, however, it is in trouble because of widespread development of the island by its human inhabitants.

SOUTH ATLANTIC ISLANDS
Endangered Birds

Raza Island lark | *Alauda razae*

Similar to the skylark of Europe except for its larger bill, this bird exists only on the tiny island of Raza, one of the Cape Verde archipelago, which lies in the South Atlantic some 300 miles off the coast of Senegal, in western Africa. An exquisite songster, the male sings in mounting flight but climbs vertically rather than in spirals—perhaps an adaptation to life on this little island, only three square miles in area. The lark may be safe while its habitat remains undisturbed, but must be considered vulnerable because of its severely limited range.

Madagascar radiated tortoise

THE OCEANS
Worlds within the World

All life, it is believed, began long ago in the ocean, that great world of water that covers more than 70 percent of the earth's surface. The diversity of life in the seas is remarkable, ranging from phytoplankton to huge sharks and giant squid, and even includes a thin tier of mammals that, like the whale, left the land at some time in the dim past to readapt themselves to a watery environment. Finding out how the creatures of the deeps and shallows are faring is not easy for air-breathing man, but we know that overfishing and pollution from human wastes have cut deeply into the aquatic populations in many areas. Because they are more visible, we know more about the mammals and reptiles that inhabit the great seas—and we know most of them are in trouble.

Bowhead whale

Vogt and Specht, *The Mammalia*

Preceding pages:
Polar bear
Gladys Porter Zoo

Endangered Mammals

Polar bear | *Thalarctos maritimus*

The spectacular polar bear can lay claim to being the largest carnivorous mammal in the world. It averages about 900 pounds—though specimens have been recorded at twice that weight—and is often more than 8 feet long. This great shaggy beast lives only in and around the Arctic Ocean, inhabiting the pack ice and feeding mainly on seals. When the floes break up in the summer it is forced to return to land, where rations are lean—roots, berries, and whatever carrion it may come upon. Powerful swimmers, polar bears are more at home in the sea than on land and have been sighted swimming along at leisure many miles from shore. When they had to contend only with Indians and Eskimos, who killed not for sport but for food, polar bears thrived. Their decline started in the seventeenth century, when the Arctic was invaded by the ships of Europeans. Their white fur was highly prized, and many were slain to become bearskin rugs. Later, when whales became scarce and the whalers turned their attention to seals, the bears found their primary food source dwindling. Modern hunters, using power boats, airplanes, and high-powered rifles, have almost succeeded in exterminating the huge animal for its fine head and shaggy coat. Belatedly, laws have been passed to protect the polar bear through most of its range, and scientists from a number of lands are trying to learn more of its habits.

Dugong | *Dugong dugon*

Like its relative the manatee, the dugong is a large, totally aquatic, herbivorous mammal. Shaped like a torpedo, it commonly grows to a length of 10 feet and a weight of almost 400 pounds. The skin, usually brownish or bluish gray, is virtually hairless, thick, and tough. Dugongs once ranged through most of the tropical seas of the Indo-Pacific area, feeding in the coastal shallows on marine vegetation and possibly shellfish. Slow in their reactions and their movements, they have been an easy prey for people of many nations. Their flesh,

Vogt and Specht, *The Mammalia*

Dugong

with a flavor resembling a cross between beef and pork, is held in high regard and is even considered an aphrodisiac by some cultures. Slaughtered mercilessly wherever they were found, dugongs disappeared from many parts of their former range in India, Ceylon, the Red Sea, Southeast Asia, and the Philippines. Their major stronghold today is around the north and east coasts of Australia, where hunting is prohibited except by aborigines, who rely on the animal as a major food source. Other countries have also passed laws protecting the dugong, but enforcement is difficult. Suggestions have been made that both the dugong and the manatee, if properly managed, could be "farmed" to become important protein sources, but little seems to have been accomplished in that direction.

Juan Fernandez fur seal | *Arctocephalus philippii philippii*

In the 1800s, immense numbers of fur seals—literally millions—inhabited the islands off the Pacific coast of South America. Then the sealers moved in, slaughtering the animals in huge numbers to meet the demands of the fur trade. One ship captain estimated that three million skins were taken in one seven-year period. Before the end of the century, the fur seal population had fallen so low that the industry was no longer profitable, and the race endemic to the Juan Fernandez archipelago was considered extinct. In 1968, however, a small colony was discovered, and the Chilean government is protecting the survivors.

Caribbean monk seal | *Monachus tropicalis*
Three widely separated species make up *Monachus,* the only seal genus to be found in warm waters: the Caribbean monk seal, the Mediterranean monk seal, and the Hawaiian monk seal, the latter so similar to the Caribbean it may be a subspecies. They may have been dubbed monk seals because of the cowllike rolls of fat behind their heads. The Caribbean monk seal was once abundant throughout the islands of the Caribbean and along the Gulf of Mexico. Slow-moving on land, and with no fear of humans, it fell easy prey to hunters and sailors seeking it for food and the oil its body contained. By the turn of the century only a few were left. Then, in 1911, a fishing party off the coast of Yucatan wiped out the last known remaining pocket of 200 animals. In later years the seal was considered extinct, but occasional sightings since 1949 of individuals and pairs give rise to hopes that the few survivors may be able to build up the population again if they are afforded adequate protection.

Hawaiian monk seal | *Monachus schauinslandi*
The silvery gray Hawaiian monk seal is limited to the Leeward Islands northwest of Hawaii, where the entire population breeds on six atolls. They flourished in this remote region for centuries, until the arrival of Western sealers in the early 1700s. The sealers slaughtered them so ruthlessly that the population was almost exterminated within the short span of fifty years. Since 1909 the seal has been protected, and most of its haunts are included in the Hawaiian Islands National Wildlife Refuge. The population has risen from fewer than 500 in 1951 to an estimated 1,500, and so long as the atolls are kept free of human intrusion the Hawaiian monk seal has a good chance of surviving into the future.

Mediterranean monk seal | *Monachus monachus*
Well known to the early Greeks and Romans, the Mediterranean monk seal formerly was distributed throughout the Mediterranean region, out to the Atlantic coast, and up into the Black Sea. This 8- or 9-foot seal, basically gray in color, often has a white ventral patch, which distinguishes it from its related species. Commercially exploited for years, the animal is no longer common, but there are enough small and medium-sized colonies scattered around the former range to ensure the survival of the seal if protective laws could be more rigidly enforced and reserves established.

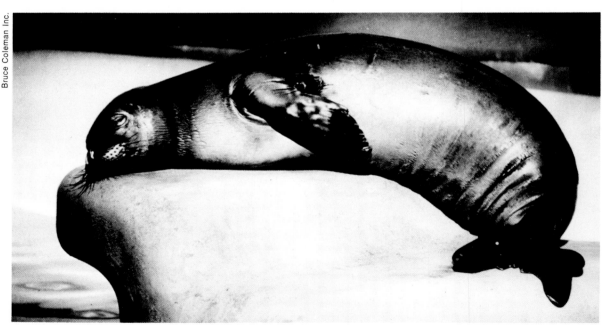

Bruce Coleman Inc.

Hawaiian monk seal

Ribbon seal | *Histriophoca fasciata*
Little is known about this 5½-foot seal, one
of the few in its family to have a distinctly
patterned coat—chocolate brown with
prominent yellowish bands around the neck
and hind quarters, with a large circle on the
side around the flippers. The ribbon seal
ranges in the northern Pacific along the eastern
coast of the USSR across the Bering Sea to
parts of Alaska. Its skin does not have much
value, and it is hunted primarily by Eskimos
and to some extent by Japanese sealers. It has
always been rare in historic times, and its
numbers have been estimated at as low as
5,000 and as high as 20,000.

Ross seal | *Ommatophoca rossi*
For many years the Ross seal, named after the
Antarctic explorer Sir John Ross, was thought
to be the rarest of the pinnipeds, for fewer than
50 specimens had been recorded by 1945,
even though expeditions to the frigid polar
regions of the south were no longer a novelty.
Today, although little is known about its habits,
it is believed to be more numerous than
previously supposed—between 20,000 and
50,000 although numbers are difficult to

estimate. The smallest of the Antarctic seals
(6½ to 8 feet and 300 to 475 pounds) and the
only one limited to Antarctic seas, it has
greenish yellow upper parts with oblique yellow
stripes on the sides, and prominent eyes that
gave rise to the early mariners' name for it:
the "big-eyed seal."

Atlantic walrus | *Odobenus rosmarus
rosmarus*
Big sea-going mammals, walruses can reach
a length of 12 feet and a weight of 3,000
pounds, with tusks as long as 3 feet. Their
thick skin is normally gray, but when they lie
basking in the sun the blood vessels dilate,
giving them a rusty appearance. They use their
tusks for levering their heavy bodies up onto
ice floes, and also for stirring up the sea
bottom where they hunt for bivalve mollusks,
their favorite food. Apparently walruses crack
open the mollusk and suck out the soft parts,
for only rarely has a shell been found in the
animal's stomach. There are two races, the
Pacific walrus, which is not currently endangered, and the Atlantic, which is. The latter
formerly ranged widely in the cold northern
seas across North America and Europe, but

overexploitation for hides, tusks, and oil resulted in their extermination on many coasts. They are protected from hunting now except by Eskimos, whose economy and welfare is based largely on the walrus, since they use just about all of the animal for food, clothing, shelter, and boat building. There are an estimated 25,000 Atlantic walruses left in Arctic waters, but with 2,500 taken every year by legal hunters, the animals may not be able to reproduce enough to maintain the population.

Whales
Despite widespread pressure from many nations of the world, the slaughter of the giant mammals of the sea continues, abating only when a species is so close to extermination that it is no longer profitable to hunt it. This happened in the nineteenth century to the right whale—just "right" in size and habits for hunting. It happened later to the huge blue whale, the largest animal the world has ever known—up to 100 feet long and 360,000 pounds in weight—which was reduced from an

estimated population of at least 150,000 to only 2,000 by 1963. It happened to the humpback whale and the bowhead whale and the gray whale, and it may happen next to the fin, sei, and sperm whales, the species most popular now with the whale catchers. Little progress has been made by those who would save the whales, for although the International Whaling Commission sets quotas on the numbers of animals that can be taken, not all countries are members of the commission. Moreover, many scientists and conservationists believe that the quotas are still so high that the remaining whale populations are steadily being depleted and will reach a point of no return sooner or later. To make matters worse, Japan, one of the two major whaling nations (Russia is the other), declared in 1973 that she would not abide by the IWC quotas and that her factory ships had a "right to harvest" as many whales as they wished. This decision was made in spite of the 53–0 vote in Stockholm in 1973 by the United Nations Environmental Conference, which called for a ten-year moratorium on whaling to allow the various species to replenish themselves. The United States has placed eight major whale species on its endangered list and has banned the importation of all products derived from them. The list includes the blue whale *(Balaenoptera musculus),* bowhead whale *(Balaena mysticetus),* humpback whale *(Megaptera novaeangliae),* right whale *(Eubalaena glacialis),* and the gray whale *(Eschrichtius robustus)*—all so overhunted that their numbers are down to the low thousands—and the fin whale *(Balaenoptera physalus),* sei whale *(Balaenoptera borealis),* and sperm whale or cachalot *(Physeter catodon),* still numerous but dwindling under heavy hunting pressure.

Fin whale
New York Public Library

Humpback whale

Lydekker, *The Royal Natural History*

Sperm whale

Vogt and Specht, *The Mammalia*

Endangered Reptiles

Hawksbill turtle | *Eretmochelys imbricata*
The smallish hawksbill, up to 36 inches long, has for years been prized for its fine "tortoise shell," the transluscent horny plates, black or brown and splotched with yellow, that cover its shell. Until driven from the market by plastic imitations, this was the tortoise shell used for Spanish combs, inlaid tables, and other costly items. In recent years, however, demand for genuine shell has been increasing, and this, together with a growing market for turtle skin as leather and hawksbill calipee—a yellowish gelatinous substance found next to the lower shield—as an ingredient in "green turtle soup," has led to a decline in the animal's population. Adding to the problem is the fact that the hawksbill apparently never moves far from its nesting beaches in the tropical and subtropical seas of its range, and therefore is coming into contact more often with spreading human populations. In the Caribbean the turtle is widely eaten, but in other areas, such as New Guinea, its flesh is considered poisonous. Also contributing to the plight of the hawksbill, which is considered the most seriously threatened of all marine turtles, is the widespread practice of killing and mounting immature specimens to be sold as curios.

Leatherback turtle | *Dermochelys coriacea*
Also called the leathery or trunkback turtle, the leatherback is the heavyweight champion of living reptiles. Specimens have been recorded at 8 feet in length and up to a ton in weight. It is easily recognized by the 7 ridges, often notched, that run lengthwise along its back under the hard, leathery skin. Its color is generally blackish on top, with irregular white or pink spots, and white underneath, with black markings. Unlike other turtles, it cannot retract its head or limbs.

Plentiful in past centuries, the leatherback ranged throughout the tropical seas and wandered as far north as Norway and as far south as Chile. As with all sea turtles, the female takes to the land after mating, moving clumsily on her flippers above the tide line to scoop out a 2-foot hole in the sand and deposit her eggs—from 6 or 8 dozen to a gross. The young hatch with no assistance, breaking the shells with their egg teeth and marching directly to the sea. Leatherbacks are not much eaten, but raids on their nests by egg collectors have seriously depleted their numbers. The only known nesting beaches today are in Costa Rica, Surinam, French Guiana, South Africa, and Malaya. This latter beach has been managed as a hatchery in recent years with good results, and another hatchery has been established in Ceylon, where the leatherback turtles once abounded.

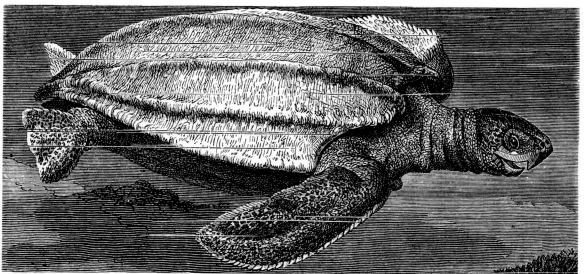

Leatherback turtle

Hawksbill turtle

BIBLIOGRAPHY

BOOKS

Thomas B. Allen. *Vanishing Wildlife of North America.* Washington, D.C.: National Geographic Society, 1974.

American Wild Life. New York: The City of New York, 1940; Wm. H. Wise and Company, 1972.

Maurice Burton, ed. *The World Encyclopedia of Animals.* New York: World Publishing Company, 1972.

Robert Burton. *The Life and Death of Whales.* New York: Universe Books, 1973.

Endangered Species. National Wildlife Federation, 1972 (paperbound).

James Fisher, Noel Simon, and Jack Vincent. *Wildlife in Danger.* New York: Viking Press and IUCN, 1969.

Gladys Porter Zoo Animal Album. Brownsville, Texas: Valley Zoological Society, 1973.

Robert Gray. *Wild World of Animals.* San Diego, California: Zoological Society of San Diego, 1973 (paperbound).

James C. Greenway, Jr. *Extinct and Vanishing Birds of the World.* New York: American Committee for International Wild Life Protection, 1958.

Francis Harper. *Extinct and Vanishing Mammals of the Old World.* New York: American Committee for International Wild Life Protection, New York Zoological Park, 1945.

The Illustrated Encyclopedia of the Animal Kingdom. Danbury Press, 1970, 1971.

Cyril Littlewood and D. W. Ovenden. *The World's Vanishing Animals.* New York: Arco Publishing Company, 1970.

Norman Myers. *The Long African Day.* New York: Macmillan Publishing Company, Inc., 1972.

The Rand McNally Atlas of World Wildlife. Chicago: Rand McNally, 1973.

Victor B. Scheffer. *A Voice for Wildlife.* New York: Charles Scribner's Sons, 1974.

Noel Simon and Paul Geroudet. *Last Survivors.* New York: World Publishing Company, 1970.

Nigel Sitwell, ed. *Animal Life '73: The World Conservation Yearbook.* Danbury Press, 1973.

Song and Garden Birds of North America. Washington, D.C.: National Geographic Society, 1964.

Threatened Wildlife of the United States. United States Department of the Interior, Resource Publication No. 114, 1973.

Ellis Troughton. *Furred Animals of Australia.* 9th ed. Sydney: Angus and Robertson, 1967.

Dr. Wolfgang Ullrich. *Endangered Species.* New York: Hart Publishing Company, 1971.

Water, Prey, and Game Birds of North America. Washington, D.C.: National Geographic Society, 1965.

World Wildlife Yearbook, 1972-73. Morges, Switzerland: World Wildlife Fund, 1973.

PERIODICALS

Africana (East African Wild Life Society)
International Wildlife
National Wildlife
Natural History
Smithsonian

ALPHABETICAL LISTING OF ENDANGERED SPECIES
Page references for illustrations are in italics.